GOING HOLLYWOOD

GOING HOLLYWOOD

How to Get Started, Keep Going and Not Turn Into a Sleaze

by Kristin M. Burke

iUniverse, Inc.
New York Lincoln Shanghai

GOING HOLLYWOOD
How to Get Started, Keep Going and Not Turn Into a Sleaze

iUniverse, Inc.

For information address:
iUniverse, Inc.
2021 Pine Lake Road, Suite 100
Lincoln, NE 68512
www.iuniverse.com

ISBN: 0-595-32495-9 (Pbk)
ISBN: 0-595-77312-5 (Cloth)

Printed in the United States of America

This book is dedicated to all people brave enough to follow their dreams.

CONTENTS

INTRODUCTION

June 18, 2004

Today, I am sitting in a large, air-conditioned office in a costume house in North Hollywood. I am designing costumes for a movie called *Running Scared*, starring Paul Walker. We leave for Prague in the Czech Republic in two days; we'll be shooting for nearly three months. It's chaos. I look around, and I think: *how in the world did I get here*?

When I graduated school and came to Los Angeles, I hit the pavement with nothing but a dream, and the knowledge that anything was possible. I had no family in the entertainment business, no fancy connections. I learned as I went—and man, did I learn a lot. I have never looked back.

There have been times that have really sucked—weeks and months that have taken the wind out of my sails. There have also been many times of triumph and joy, participating in the creation of something significant that will outlast me. This business is not easy, but I have come to love it, warts and all.

When asked for advice to young people coming to Hollywood, Bette Davis once simply said, "Take Fountain…," but I would like to do better than that. I would like to give you the book that I wish I had when I arrived. Hopefully, it will prove insightful and useful to you on your journey.

Best of luck and good wishes~

Kristin M. Burke

OVERVIEW

This book is a path to getting an entertainment career started in Hollywood. This is specifically *not* a book for actors. The actor's path is another book in itself; one that I am not qualified to write. Having a successful entertainment career, whether in production, management, development, distribution, or industry support, is an attainable and achievable goal. There are some clear guidelines to follow, and there is a logical, although sometimes jagged, order to successful progress.

This book should not serve as a deciding factor in your pursuit of an entertainment career. You need to be sure that the entertainment business is something about which you are truly passionate. Entertainment should feel like your "calling". To really succeed, the calling to the entertainment industry must be one that appears beyond your control. To a great extent, this business chooses *you.*

WHAT DOES IT TAKE TO MAKE IT IN THE ENTERTAINMENT FIELD?

Endurance and perseverance are essential to a long and productive life in Hollywood. The obvious asset is TALENT, but there are plenty of less-talented people who work more, earn more, and are more famous than those endowed with jaw-dropping gifts. What makes one person succeed over another? People who have succeeded, and continue to succeed, in this business share a number of common traits:

1) <u>Drive</u>
   Drive; not ambition. Drive is a constant, steady impulse. Ambition is passive and goal-oriented. Drive compels you and motivates you to achievement; ambition is merely a *desire* for fame, power, or money. You will need more than desire to achieve anything in Hollywood. Positive attitude and killer instinct play an important role in expressing your drive. Let your positive attitude be killer instinct wearing a nice dress. Image is very important in Hollywood, and the blatant, more aggressive "killer instinct" types tend to be regarded as a nuisance, distasteful and undesirable. It is so easy to put a nice face on your killer instinct. Let your smiling drive propel you forward.

2) Faith
You must know, beyond doubt, that you will be successful. You can't hope, pray, wish, dream of being successful, you must KNOW that you will be. It may not happen tomorrow, or next year, but *eventually* you will triumph—and you must know it. Faith in your own ability and confidence in your quest are tremendous and necessary assets. No matter how many setbacks you encounter, no matter how persuasive an argument can be made for quitting, your faith in yourself and your reason for being here must sustain you through difficult times. Be strong.

3) Vision
Foresight, imagination, and invention are powerful tools in the creation of entertainment. Despite the franchise movement in the film industry, Hollywood still loves new ideas. Hollywood even loves old ideas wrapped in new paper. Innovation can be your key to success. Ingenious new takes on old themes, creative problem solving, or technological advances in your field can make you millions. Wouldn't you liked to have invented IMAX or CG Animation?! Be ready to think on your feet.

4) Tenacity
Competition in the industry is fierce—sometimes it is up-front and aggressive, sometimes it is disturbingly subtle and insidious. But, like the last man sitting on the flagpole, tenacity is something that can bring you success when you have tried everything else, and exhausted all of your options. A competitive edge is necessary for any placement in this industry; there is no sidestepping the fight. If you give up, you lose. Persistence pays off.

5) Patience
Patience is a virtue that very few people in Los Angeles like to discuss. This is a fast-moving place, and when results are not immediate, they are perceived to be non-existent. The development of a career in the entertainment industry takes time. With limited exception, nothing happens overnight. Working in a technical or behind-the-scenes field, count on eight years of hard work before you can see results of your professional and personal efforts. A successful entertainment career is the process of consistent achievement and excellence in your field. Stay focused, and be patient.

6) Balls
Most importantly, you will need big brass balls. It may seem uncouth to discuss the need for balls, but really there is no synonym. Chutzpah, gumption, boldness—these words simply do not do justice to what you will need to really

make it. You need balls, friends. Let's break it down, to be specific: courage, gall, cheekiness, bravery, flamboyance, shock value, brilliance, tempered arrogance, daring, pluck, nerve, guts—all of this and more comprises "balls". Bold presentation and brilliant salesmanship can go very, very far in Hollywood. You may not (and should not) need or use your balls every day, but boy, when you need them you'd better use them. Seize your opportunities.

All of the above are developed sets of behavioral traits. If you don't already possess them, you should work to build up these areas in your personality before coming to Los Angeles. You will then have these strengths to bolster your pursuit and to carry you through hard times in Hollywood.

THE DIFFERENCE BETWEEN LOS ANGELES AND HOLLYWOOD

Los Angeles is a catchall name for the area of land within roughly a ten-mile radius of the intersection of Beverly Boulevard and La Cienega Boulevard. There are independently incorporated cities within this zone, including Santa Monica, West Hollywood, and Beverly Hills. The rest of the areas in town are known by their neighborhood names: Brentwood, Holmby Hills, Mar Vista, Larchmont, Carthay Circle, Beachwood, Koreatown, Echo Park, and so forth.

Hollywood is not only a neighborhood; it is a concept. *Hollywood* can be defined as the entertainment industry, or the characteristics of one who works in the entertainment industry. "Going Hollywood" signifies not only a commitment to the business, but a shift in perception. To "Go Hollywood" is to dive in to the entertainment industry and immerse oneself in the culture.

WHAT IS IT LIKE TO LIVE IN LOS ANGELES?

Los Angeles and its environs are some of the most beautiful, colorful and diverse places in this country. We have mountains, beaches, freeways, rivers, skyscrapers, and golf courses all within a few hundred square miles. This is the place where dreams can come true. Millions of people come here every year from all over the world in pursuit of those dreams, making our city a phenomenal melting pot of culture, language, music and open-mindedness. Present-day Los Angeles has been compared to Renaissance-age Florence, and while that may seem an implausibly flattering comparison, consider our current placement in the pop-culture world. Hollywood is this country's breeding ground for cultural change and artistic evolution through entertainment. An invigorating place to live, Los Angeles *does* have its idiosyncrasies. What is it like, then, to live here?

1) Traffic

Los Angeles is a sprawling mass of construction that goes on for forty miles in any direction. This large area of land was developed *after* the invention of the automobile. Development spread *outward* (to the drivable suburbs), rather than upward (like New York City), and the city spreads out for an eternity. With twelve million inhabitants on these roads, traffic can be a bit of a challenge. In morning and afternoon rush hours, the Los Angeles area freeways are a congested mass of steel and frustration. Since the presence of public transportation is very limited, most people own cars and drive themselves where they need to go. People display varying degrees of courtesy on the road. If you are involved in a collision, be reminded that this is a litigious society, and the threat of lawsuits is close to the surface. Drive carefully.

2) Smog

One side effect of all of those cars is smog. It is said in Los Angeles that "you are what you drive". You would never guess that there are so many bloated, fuel-hungry behemoths out there, but by the looks of our freeways, we've been invaded. The ensuing smog can wreak havoc on your skin and lungs. Those with asthma be warned: carry your inhaler. Smog levels are greatly improved since our parents' generation, but you will still see a thick layer of brown crud settled over the lower-lying areas of our city. Smog is generally worse in the summer (the sun is more intense, and the smog-creating chemical reactions more readily occur), but it is present all year round in Los Angeles.

3) Cost of Living

Living in Los Angeles will cost less than living in New York, Tokyo or San Francisco, but it is still expensive. Rent has become a sore point lately, and it has become expensive to live alone in an apartment. The price of homes has risen to heights that were truly inconceivable ten years ago. We may be in for a "correction" in the next few years, but it is still pricey. You may find only a slight variation in the prices for groceries, books, music, and basic supplies from what you currently pay in your hometown. However, you may experience sticker shock at some of the prices here for gas (petrol), automobile repair, haircuts, cigarettes, cab fare, drinks at a bar, and so forth. Prepare to spend more than you are accustomed.

4) People

The people in Los Angeles are an interesting bunch. For the most part, people relocate here because they are a) pursuing their dreams of working in the entertainment industry, b) are in search of better weather, c) fleeing an oppressive foreign regime, or d) are working for JPL, oil companies, or other Los Angeles-based mega-corporations. There are, of course, a very few native Angelenos here. If you are working in the entertainment industry, most people you will encounter are originally from somewhere else.

There are many "types" that emerge from the people working in entertainment who have made the long trek from Timbuktoo, Big City X, Foreign Country A, or even Encino. You will not be able to swing a dead cat without hitting a) social climbers, b) plastic surgery victims, c) vapid, gold-digging superficialists, d) wannabes, e) big bad egomaniacal superstars, f) control freaks, g) self-proclaimed geniuses, h) divas with agendas, i) sleaze-balls, and j) Satan impersonators. That being said, there are an awful lot of genuinely nice, kind people in Los Angeles. In order to survive, you will need to develop a discerning eye that will enable you to steer clear of even the most ingenious Satan impersonator.

Culturally speaking, the ethnic makeup of this city is as diverse as it gets. Although the city is fairly well integrated, ethnic neighborhoods still exist, and you can hear many languages spoken fluently within one block. This place is a wonderful melting pot, not only adding energy to the idea that dreams can come true, but also underlining the value and importance of personal freedom.

5) Urban Sprawl

The city goes on forever, and the freeways never stop humming. There is no escape from noise. It is a fact about Los Angeles that few people talk about—the complete and utter lack of silence. We have all acclimated to it, and tend not to notice how constant the noise it, all of the day and most of the night.

Open space and nature at first glance appears to be in short supply, but only to the uninitiated. There are many beautiful parks and preserves around town, which are detailed chapter #5 in this book. These places serve as a wonderful touchstone of perspective for all Angelenos, reminding us that despite all of our skyscrapers and freeways, we are really a part of nature.

6) Weather

It is almost always a nice day in Los Angeles. The highest temperature ever recorded at the Los Angeles Civic Center was 112°F, in June 1990. The lowest temperature ever recorded at the Los Angeles Civic Center was 28°F, in January 1949. The average number of wet-weather days per year in Los Angeles is 35. Average annual rainfall is just less than fifteen inches. The last time it snowed in

Los Angeles was 1962, and even then, only trace amounts.[1] The seasons change, but almost imperceptibly. You can wear shorts, flip-flops, and sunscreen year-round. Your car will not get salt-damaged. Your swimming pool will never freeze. You can plant just about anything in your garden. It's a beautiful thing.

7) <u>Endless Possibilities</u>
One of the most inspiring things about Los Angeles is the feeling that anything is possible, and that self-reinvention or self-improvement is attainable. This is the land where dreams can come true (and conversely, can be shattered), and the feeling of endless possibility here is pervasive. This is an exuberant and lively place with a sense of personal freedom that is very rare. Personal expression is widely encouraged, and nothing is ever really very shocking. Blue Mohawk? We have thirty-five of 'em. Full body tattoos? Eyelid piercings? Seen it, done it, NEXT! A conservative society this is not.

WHAT IS IT LIKE TO HAVE A CAREER IN THE INDUSTRY?

Every person has a different story about how they started. Every person has a different perspective on how life in Los Angeles, and in the business, has shaped and changed them. In the beginning, though, for most people, it is a chug-chug-chugging kind of existence, working hard, building up speed and learning the ropes, ramping up for the first peak. After the first peak, there is always the first valley or plateau. It can often feel like a roller-coaster ride: exhilarating one moment and devastating the next. The important thing to know is that you do not have to be a backbiting, workaholic sleaze-ball to be successful.

There are plenty of sleaze-balls who have made millions at the box office, whose lives are empty and sad because nothing good can grow inside them. You need only look to the success of Steven Spielberg, Tom Hanks, Ron Howard and those like them in this industry to know that success without sleaze is possible.

If you are in this industry for the right reason, the reason being a "calling", it never really feels like work. If you start to question what you're doing here, if you start to hate it, if your lifestyle begins to become destructive to your health or if it causes you to become destructive or dangerous to others, get out. This business is not for everyone, and you will need to develop strengths to weather its storms.

ARE YOU STILL WITH ME?

---

1 Source: National Weather Service, Los Angeles Almanac: <u>www.losangelesalmanac.com</u>

INTERVIEW

Subject: Jennifer Sanger
Executive, DreamWorks

Hometown: Albany, OR
Moved to LA: 1991

Topic: Making the Move

Where did you attend college & what did you study?

I attended Oregon State University and studied English Literature. However, in my Junior year, our Liberal Arts department saw major budget cuts and the English department took a serious hit. It was impossible to get into the upper-level classes needed to complete the degree, so the Liberal Arts department created a Liberal Studies degree which allowed students to cross over into other Liberal Arts concentrations—the idea being to individualize our areas of concentration. Besides English classes, I was able to take classes in film, theatre, history and art. That is where I got my first taste for production—working on a film (i.e. a student film) and a theatre production.

Did you always want to work in the entertainment industry?

No. I seriously thought I was going to be an advertising executive a la Courtney Thorne Smith on *Melrose Place*. I moved to L.A. thinking I'd look for work at an advertising agency. But, after living in my brother's dining room for 2 months and having a hard time finding a job, my brother urged me to work as a P.A. on one of his girlfriend's movies. The rest is history.

When did you decide to move to LA, and why?

Spring break my freshman year. I made a trip to L.A. with my parents to visit my brother and fell in love.

What were you most afraid of, making the move?

I was fearless. I felt as though I had nothing to lose.

How did it go?

It went great. After the first 2 months of not working, I worked steadily for the next year. I was able to move into my own place after 6 months of crashing with my brother, made lots of great friends and some good work contacts.

What were some of the hardest things to adjust to when you moved to LA?

I felt like I hatched when I moved to L.A. I can't really think of anything that was hard for me to adjust to. I completely savored every moment of my "adjustment". I enjoyed soaking in the newness of living outside of Oregon and meeting interesting people. I probably wished I had more money. In college I could go out for the night with $5.00 in my pocket. In LA, $5 wouldn't even buy you one drink in a bar.

Describe your first job:

I was a (horrible) Production Assistant on Roger Corman's *Little Miss Millions* starring Howard Hessman and Jennifer Love Hewitt. My brother's girlfriend got me the job. On my first day, I couldn't believe I was asked to pick up garbage and wait until every single crew person got a plate of food from the caterer before I got in line. I had a big wake-up call that very day. Soon after, maybe one or two movies later, I was asked to P.A. in the office. That was a great move for me!

How long did it take before you found yourself in a career path that you love?

It took me about a year and a half. After working on 3 films at Roger Corman's studio, Concorde-New Horizons, I was asked to coordinate a film. I had no idea what I was doing and had very little training. After about 6 months there, I went on to do a few independent pictures with other production companies. Then I found myself out of work for several months, so I started temping. I found a temp agency that placed at entertainment companies and advertising agencies so I worked with them for a while. I thought I might be able to get in the door with a company (either film-related or advertising) and work my way up. I was sick of freelancing. I got a job updating rolodexes at CAA, which was a blast, but then I was asked to coordinate a picture with a UPM (Unit Production Manager) I had worked with previously. I made the decision to give production another chance and somehow it really clicked with me. I haven't looked back.

Is there anything you would have done differently?

Probably not. I sometimes wonder where I'd be if I hadn't taken this staff job at DreamWorks 8 years ago. I'm really happy where I am, but I think everyone wonders "what if?" at some time in their life. I look at the bright side. I probably wouldn't have met my husband if I hadn't taken this job!

You say the job at DreamWorks also brought you your husband—how did that work?

Well, when DreamWorks first started, there were a lot of people my age that worked in close proximity. We all became fast friends and hung out together a lot outside of the workplace. One Friday night I met one of my co-workers out, he introduced us and the rest is history.

Any advice for people wanting to make the move & start their career?

The best pieces of advice I can give are: be persistent and don't give up. Make as many contacts as possible. Once you've developed a relationship with a trusty contact, ask that person to put you in touch with 2 more potential contacts. Buy a Thomas Guide and learn the city. Learn how to be savvy and practice finesse. And finally, be flexible—especially when you're starting out. You may be offered a job you don't think you want, but don't be too quick to turn it down. You never know what opportunity might present itself or who you might meet.

CHAPTER ONE

GETTING READY

WHAT TO TELL YOUR FAMILY

You have thought about it for a long time. You have made a decision to move and change your life. You have made this decision because you are at one of the following crossroads: a) recently graduated from high school, college, or grad school, or b) having a mid-life crisis/seeking a life change. The good part is that you have figured it out and made the decision. The occasionally hard part is telling your family.

They will be scared of Los Angeles—"It's such a big city! The riots! The crime! The gangs!"—they are not wrong to be scared for your safety. This can be a rough place, but you will learn (if you haven't already) the street-smarts to get you through. They will also probably state (and I am paraphrasing) "Honey, we know you have the talent, but we just don't trust the INDUSTRY"—and this is also valid. However, more likely than not, your family doesn't know bubkus about how the industry works.

Most importantly, you need to make sure that YOU know how the industry works! If you haven't had the benefit of college-level curriculum in filmmaking, television production, or talent management, get thyself to the library immediately. There are hundreds of books written about how this business works, and it is imperative that you have a grasp on what it is you are pursuing. You may want to peruse websites including www.aintitcool.com, www.chud.com, www.imdb.com, www.eonline.com, www.filmjerk.com, www.joebobbriggs.com, www.rottentomatoes.com, www.zentertainment.com—all of which offer interesting insight into the entertainment business. Educate yourself; you will not regret it. That being said:

Step number one: Educate your family about the workings of the film industry.
This is primarily done through books, NOT through People Magazine or Project Greenlight. Go to the bookstore and get a few basic books on how films are made—from the development process to the distribution process. Give them to your family as gifts that they can keep and to which they may refer in the future. Read them yourself first so you can speak a common language. Demystify the filmmaking process. Pick up the Daily Variety and The Hollywood Reporter and share them with your family. If they have firmly preconceived notions of Machiavellian practices of studio bosses and sleazy casting couches, you may not be able to do much to affect their opinions, but you can at least make the effort.

Step number two: Remind your family of your passion for your field, and of your calling for the industry.
If your family understands you, and if they really know you, this will be a no-brainer. However, many parents want stable lives for their children, skills and talent aside. Parents sometimes forget, or aren't aware of, their child's passions. It is worthwhile to discuss your reasons for wanting a career in entertainment in any case—good communication will ease any transition.

Step number three (last resort): The "Life is Short/One Shot" lecture.
This is meant for the worst-case scenario, featuring the possibility of a disinheritance, long estrangement or major fight. The "Life is Short/One Shot" lecture (in short) is comprised of the following points: 1) Life is short and it could all be over tomorrow, 2) I get one shot at life, one chance to create my opportunities, 3) I must seize these opportunities while I have the strength and the ability to capitalize on them, 4) If I don't pursue my passion, I will spend the rest of my life wondering what I could have become, 5) I believe in myself and I owe it to myself to try. Use your own words, or borrow heavily from Eminem's hit "Lose Yourself"—the message will be clear. If your family remains very firmly against your decision, it is up to *you* to decide whose life you will lead.

A word to parents reading this book: don't crucify your kids for choosing a life in the entertainment industry. The business is hard enough as it is with good support, not to mention disapproval. Condescension and disparaging remarks are not going to change your child's mind; they will only inspire profound resentment. Trust your child's judgment and stay in his/her life. They will need you for moral support. Know where your wishes for your child end and where their lives begin. They will thank you in their acceptance speech.

MOVING FORWARD AND MAKING PLANS

Before you do anything, you will need to scour your world for contacts. Ask your family and friends if they know anyone in Los Angeles with whom you can talk about work options. Failing that, search for helpful contacts through your University Alumni network, religious congregation, fraternity or sorority organizations, philanthropic associations, anything. Having even just one person to talk to when you arrive in Los Angeles can be a great source of comfort. If you can't find even one soul in Los Angeles through this method, never fear. You will meet people along the way.

If you are fresh out of school and have never had a job before, you may find that the easiest way to start your entertainment career is through interning or apprenticing. This may or may not pay—you may have to work for free. However, the contacts and the hands-on experience that you are able to get as a result will be invaluable. Even if you have a graduate degree, you may need to start out apprenticing. Swallow your pride and get over it. Advanced degrees do not make or break a job candidate in the entertainment industry.

If you are coming from a foreign country, you will need to have a work permit or a work visa issued by the US Government. You will not be permitted to be *paid to work* in this country unless you hold a work permit, work visa, or a green card…no matter how good your English is. You *can*, however, work as an unpaid intern or apprentice. The entertainment industry is a wonderful training ground, and if you can afford to <u>not</u> be paid, you can intern here.

You would be well-advised to send out resumes to production companies and/or agencies a month before you decide to move to Los Angeles. If you want to work in one of the technical aspects of film production, pick up a Tuesday edition of the <u>Hollywood Reporter</u>, or a Friday edition of the <u>Daily Variety</u>—both publications list films in production and preparation, along with contact names and addresses/phone numbers. If you want to work in television, pick up the Thursday edition of the <u>Daily Variety</u> or the first-and-third-Tuesday editions of the <u>Hollywood Reporter</u>—both will have production company name and phone numbers listed. With production jobs, it is always best to call first and speak with a Production Coordinator to find out if they are hiring/accepting resumes. If you would like to work in development, send resumes to the production companies themselves—call first and get a contact name of someone in Human Resources, speak to them if you can, and set up a nice, friendly rapport. If you want to work in Talent Management or Representation, send resumes to the agencies themselves, again getting in touch with someone from

Human Resources and having a nice chat. You might be able to get a foot in the door with a company by requesting an informational interview (as opposed to a real job interview) to familiarize yourself with the way they do business.

In researching apartments, a quick and easy head-start would be to visit either www.apartmentsource.com or www.westsiderentals.com. These are apartment-, house-, and roommate-finder websites for the entire Los Angeles area. You can search by price, location, or whether or not pets are accepted. It costs money to join these services, but your membership will last you months. You can browse for potential apartments before you make your preliminary visit to Los Angeles, and save yourself some time in the process.

You also might want to think about subletting an apartment until you sort yourself out in the city. Subletting an apartment is usually cheaper than renting one, and you can make arrangements for a sublet to last a few weeks, or a few months, depending on availability. Along these lines, you can occasionally find a furnished bedroom to rent for a short time, very similar to a sublet. There are a few websites you might try in this vein. They include: www.sublet.com, and www.cho.ucla.edu. The former is a web-based service (for a fee) that covers many big cities, including Los Angeles. The latter is the UCLA housing board, which is free, and lists apartments and sublets in and around the Westwood campus of UCLA.

In preparing for your life in Los Angeles, you should make sure to have the following: a cell phone, or several calling cards (to keep long-distance family and friends in the loop), web-based email address (such as yahoo or Hotmail), a minimum of fifteen copies of your resume, a minimum of $5,000 in accessible funds, and a reliable motorcycle or automobile.

Why so much money?!? You can probably get to Los Angeles with $50 and a Greyhound bus ticket, but I wouldn't recommend it. The $5000 is not an arbitrary amount. For starters, you will need money to secure an apartment. Most places require first month's rent, last (final) month's rent and security deposit to be paid in full before you can take possession of the keys. If your apartment rents for $1000/month, that's $1,000 (first month's rent), plus $1000 (final month's rent), plus conservatively $750 (security deposit); you are looking at $2750 just to set up your apartment. Add to that home phone, cell phone, cable, and utilities set-up, plus first month's living expenses (including food, gas, business expenses), and your $5,000 goes up in smoke. Anything additional that you can save from that amount should be put in a savings account for a rainy day, or for a time where you may be out-of-work and need to live off of it. You can come to Los Angeles with less money in your pocket, but you severely limit your options.

Do I really need a reliable motorcycle or automobile? YES. The City of Los Angeles has some of the saddest mass transit in the country. We have a bus system that runs city-wide, but you will need eight million schedules, sixty-five bus route maps, and a master's degree in engineering to figure it out. There is the metro system of light rail and commuter trains, but unless you work downtown, it is useless. Thus, the need for your own transportation. Since Los Angeles is so sprawling, bicycling is difficult. Further, it is hazardous—drivers here are not accustomed to cyclists or pedestrian traffic. You can buy a used car for easily under $3,000 when you get here, but have a good mechanic in your neighborhood at the ready. We all depend on our cars for work, and you may be asked to *use* your car for work (making deliveries, runs, etc.). In the end, you will be glad you have a dependable car. If getting a car or motorcycle is out of the question financially, realize that your freedom will be extremely limited. Make getting a vehicle your #1 priority.

Once those elements are in place, you are prepared to make the exploratory Los Angeles trip, the SCOUT. Plan on coming to Los Angeles for about three days to look for an apartment, interview for a job, and/or register with a temp agency.

You may need help when you make the move to Los Angeles, either from friends or family. If you are unable to enlist the help of friends and family, do not fret; it is still possible—but be prepared for the schlepping. If your family is still feeling anxious about your move, let them help. It may make them feel better, as they can have their own experience of the city, and perhaps feel more comfortable with your decision.

INTERVIEW

Subject: Anurag Mehta
Writer/Director, ***American Chai***

Hometown: Cherry Hill, NJ
Moved to LA: 1995

Topic: Familial pressure & forging your own path

Where did you attend college & what did you study?

I went to Rutgers College in New Brunswick, New Jersey. I was a finance major. Even though I've loved movies my entire life, it wasn't until my sophomore year at college that I decided I wanted to pursue film for real. I went to the administration to see if I could switch my major, but they only offered Cinema as a major for students enrolled in their art school. If I transferred I would have had to lose a year or so...and so I ended up keeping my finance major and minoring in Cinema Studies. I still got to take all the same classes as the Cinema majors so it didn't really matter. I put all my effort into the film classes and just kind of skated through the finance classes...not recommended as a good way to go through college...

Did your parents have expectations of you for your career that conflicted with your desire to be in film production?

Well, I remember they were initially happy that I decided to keep my major as finance...But soon, when they realized that film wasn't just a passing hobby, then they became very supportive. My parents have their own real estate company in Southern New Jersey, and I'm sure at some point they would've loved for me or my brother to take it over, but once they realized that our dreams were elsewhere (my brother is an actor and a musician; he plays the lead in *American Chai*), they stopped counting on us to take over the family business...

When did you decide to move to LA, & did you have a plan?

After our junior year at college, two of my best friends were going to LA to be interns at film companies during summer break. I decided to join them and all of us came out here and got a place together for the summer. We all scored great internships...I ended up working as a development intern for James Cameron. It wasn't your typical Hollywood internship, as they took it pretty seriously at his company, Lightstorm. I had some real responsibilities and I really learned a tremendous amount. Plus, I got to attend some great screenings, industry parties, etc. And the fact that I had the chance to interact with somebody like James Cameron (whom I'm a big fan of) was amazing. The whole experience was my first brush with the industry and I loved it. And being with my friends, I had the time of my life.

Then I went back to Jersey to finish my senior year at Rutgers. It was right around the time when *Pulp Fiction* had come out, and *Clerks* and *El Mariachi* and the whole "indie" scene was just starting up. I was inspired by Quentin Tarantino, Kevin Smith and Robert Rodriguez and right after graduation I, too, wanted to make a small film on a shoestring budget...except my plan was to shoot it in India. I had some connections in Bollywood and you know, the dollar goes a long way over there. But, ultimately, I decided I wasn't ready to undergo such a major endeavor just yet, so instead I joined my two friends that I had spent the previous summer with, and we all moved to Los Angeles to pursue careers in film.

I was already familiar with the industry after having done my internship, so my plan was to get an entry-level job at a production company to pay the bills and gain experience, while working on my screenplays in my free time.

How did you tell your family (and extended family), and what did you tell them?

Of course my parents were not happy about me moving 3000 miles away...but I have to say, I'm very lucky because my parents never insisted on what I did...instead they insisted on how I did it. If I was going to do something, I better put my all into it and work hard and take it extremely seriously. They understood that a career in Hollywood required moving to Hollywood, so they were supportive.

My extended family (and I have a very large one) was a different story. Most of them were cool, but a few of my uncles and aunts...let's just say I would get a lot of questions, and though no one really came out and said it, it didn't take an FBI profiler to figure out that they didn't quite approve of what I was doing.

What were their concerns?

What ended up happening for me, was that some of my extended family expressed their concerns to my parents, not to me, and my parents ended up defending us (my brother and I). Someone in my family even wrote a letter to my father urging him to force me to move back home to Jersey and take over the business.

I think I understand the roots of their concerns, though I do not agree with them. I come from an immigrant family. My parents and my extended family, they are all immigrants from India, now settled in the U.S. It's not the case for all of them, but a great many of the Indian immigrants from the 1960's and 1970's tend to have a very conservative outlook on life. It is certainly true of my extended family. And for some of them, they have a very negative view of the entertainment industry. They live G-rated lives (at least publicly), and the film biz is an R-rated world...

Also, immigrants, as a whole, have a certain mindset, understandably. Though their individual reasons for leaving their homelands may vary, they all share one common trait—they all came here in pursuit of opportunity, in pursuit of something better than they had at home…whether it was education, or work, or both. And they sacrificed a lot by coming here. It's not an easy thing that they did. So, naturally, when you sacrifice so much for an opportunity, you are not going to take it for granted…you are going to make the absolute most of it. And to them, pursuing a career in the arts isn't quite making the most of your opportunity. It's extremely risky. The odds of making it are slim. There are much better ways to make a living.

I can't stress how fortunate I am that my parents understood that their children having the freedom to pursue their dreams is exactly the kind of opportunity they came to America for…Also, my parents understand the artistic impulses that someone can have, which a lot of people don't "get". If my goal was just to make money and live comfortably, I would not be doing this. I have an inherent drive to express myself artistically. It's a human quality. It's not something alien. But if you're not familiar with it, and you've never been exposed to it, it could be difficult to comprehend.

Describe your first living arrangement:

As I mentioned, I moved out here with two of my best friends. We ended up getting a three bedroom place together in Westwood. We picked Westwood because of the movie theaters. We all shared a common love for the movies. The theaters in LA, especially in Westwood, are the best. The sound and picture quality is always first-rate, and the audiences are so vocal and appreciative…I really think it's the place in the world to see a movie. So my friends and I would try and have that experience as many times as possible. The summers were the best, because you had a big movie opening every weekend…and if it was something good, we'd see it over and over again.

It was an amazing time in my life, and one I miss very much. Lots of fond memories. We all had industry jobs and we all wrote our screenplays in our free time. Many many late nights, lots of trips to Vegas, and a few things that I can't talk about…

Describe your first job:

Speaking of things I can't talk about…you know the movie *Swimming with Sharks*? I cried when I saw that, because that was my life. I totally related to that movie one hundred percent. About a week into my first job, I quickly realized that my internship with James Cameron the summer before was a fantasy that had spoiled me. The job I got when I moved back here was the quintessential

Hollywood "personal assistant" job. The verbal abuse I endured became as routine as my morning coffee. It was for a big-time Hollywood producer from back in the day. Even though it was the 'Nineties, he was still maintaining his 70's life of excess. And somehow, I paid the price. I lasted about a year. I could probably fill up this entire book with crazy stories. Some were downright hell. Believe it or not, it's been eight years, and I still have nightmares about it. On the bright side, I did learn a lot about myself and life during that period.

But the way I got the job was similar to the way many others get their jobs out here. There is something called the UTA list...UTA is the United Talent Agency, and they compile a list of all open positions in the industry. I think it's updated every couple of weeks, if not more than that. It's one of these things that floats around town and you have to work a little to get your hands on it. I was able to get one from a friend and basically, I called all the openings on the list. The other useful tool for getting a job out here is the Creative Directory. That costs some money, but it's a listing of every production company in town. I borrowed a friend's, went through it and cold-called a hundred companies. It took about 4 or 5 weeks to do it, but eventually I arranged some interviews and landed the job.

Despite the issues I had with that first job, the offices were on a studio lot and that made it exciting. Everyday I'd walk by movie sets, and directors and stars...it was pretty cool.

How difficult was your adjustment to life in LA?

The crazy job made it much more difficult to adjust. My days were sometimes downright miserable, and that made me miss my family and friends back home all the more. The saving grace was that I was living with my two best friends. I think we all made it easier for each other to adjust to life away from our families.

But in general, LA isn't a hard place to adjust to. The weather's always beautiful, there is so much to do, and if you love movies as much as I do, then it really is the place to be.

How does your family feel about your life in entertainment now that you have made your mark, and can you talk about the parallels with *American Chai* subject matter?

American Chai is about an Indian-American college student who hides his rock & roll aspirations from his strict immigrant parents...Naturally, everyone always asks me if Chai is based on my own life, my own parents, my own upbringing. My Dad definitely foresaw this because he told me right away after seeing the film...make sure you tell everyone that I'm not like the Dad in the movie!

But even though my own parents are much more supportive than the parents in the film, I drew from a lot of real situations taking place around me. Whether it was my friends, or cousins, or whomever...the central conflict in the movie is definitely very truthful. I may not have clashed with my folks about my career choice, but I did have other things that I had trouble telling them about...so the gist of the movie is really about communication. Try to deal with your issues through communication. A lot of people have drawn this from the movie and that's very satisfying...even members of my family.

Once they saw the finished film, I definitely got some love from family that was very genuine and touching. Family is a funny thing, they will voice their concerns, they will sometimes discourage you, but there is authentic love at the core of their actions. And I felt that love from a lot of people after my film came out. I know I'm lucky to have had that, because it's rare that people express such things. After my film came out, people started sharing their feelings with me in a way they didn't do before.

The funny thing is, now everyone wants to know when the next movie is coming out...It's not easy, I'm working on it!

If you were to do it again, what would you do differently?

I've never been one to look back at the past with any sort of regret or anything like that. Part of it is trying to make choices now that I hope I won't regret in the future...but of course, there are lessons one can learn from the past.

One thing I would tell a young person that might be thinking about a career in Hollywood is to consider going to film school in LA. It's something I didn't do, and I sometimes wonder about it. I'm certainly able to learn everything there is to learn about film from my own education and experience, but the one thing I find I'm lacking, when compared to people that went to film school here in LA, is the networking. Their entire school body more or less stayed in LA and moved on to work here in the industry. There is a tremendous amount of networking that goes on there (in film school) that can be very beneficial. For that reason, I sometimes wish that I had known what I wanted to do with my life just a little bit earlier...

But like I said...I'm not one to regret things. Everything happens exactly the way it's supposed to happen. You have to play the cards you're dealt!

Anything else you'd like to add?

When I first started making my film, a fellow filmmaker who had already had success with his first film told me to never, ever, give up on my project under any circumstances. I found that to be very valuable advice that helped carry me through the sometimes taxing experience of making a first feature. So for anyone that is still reading this interview, I would like to just say—stay positive. It's very easy to see the negatives, because even if you don't see the negatives yourself, I guarantee that someone will point them out to you. So you must find the positives. Hold on to them. Protect them. That's what gets you through.

CHAPTER TWO

WELCOME TO H'WOOD

SCOUTING LA, AND SETTING YOURSELF UP

You've decided to come to Los Angeles for the Scout. If you can't stay with friends, book a reasonably-priced hotel. Reasonably-priced in Los Angeles is relative; you'd be hard-pressed to find a good room for less than $85/night. If you are flying in from out of town, you will need to rent a car. Before you leave, make sure you Mapquest or YahooMap driving directions from the airport to your hotel/friend's house. Print the directions out and carry them in your wallet. The two convenient area airports are LAX (in Inglewood) and Burbank International (in Burbank). Jet Blue and some other discount airlines fly into John Wayne Airport in Long Beach, which is a 30-mile drive that can take up to an hour, but if it saves you money, do it.

First order of business: Get a newspaper. Local newspapers here include the Los Angeles Times, the Daily Breeze, and the Daily News. The Daily Breeze, Daily News, the Recycler, and the (Santa Monica) Outlook will all have apartment and home rental information in their classified section.

CRAIG'S LIST

You can also find information about housing, jobs, community events, and more in the craig's list website for Angelenos: http://losangeles.craigslist.org/. With regard to housing, they list rooms for rent, share, sublet, along with commercial space rental, and a place for posting "housing wanted". You can buy or sell a car, Dodger tickets, pets, give away or take home free goods and so on through this site; it operates much like the classifieds. Alternatively, check out the apartment rental websites www.westsiderentals.com, www.apartmentsource.com, www.sublet.com, or www.cho.ucla.edu, if you didn't before you left. Now is the time to drive through the neighborhoods and figure out where you'd like to live.

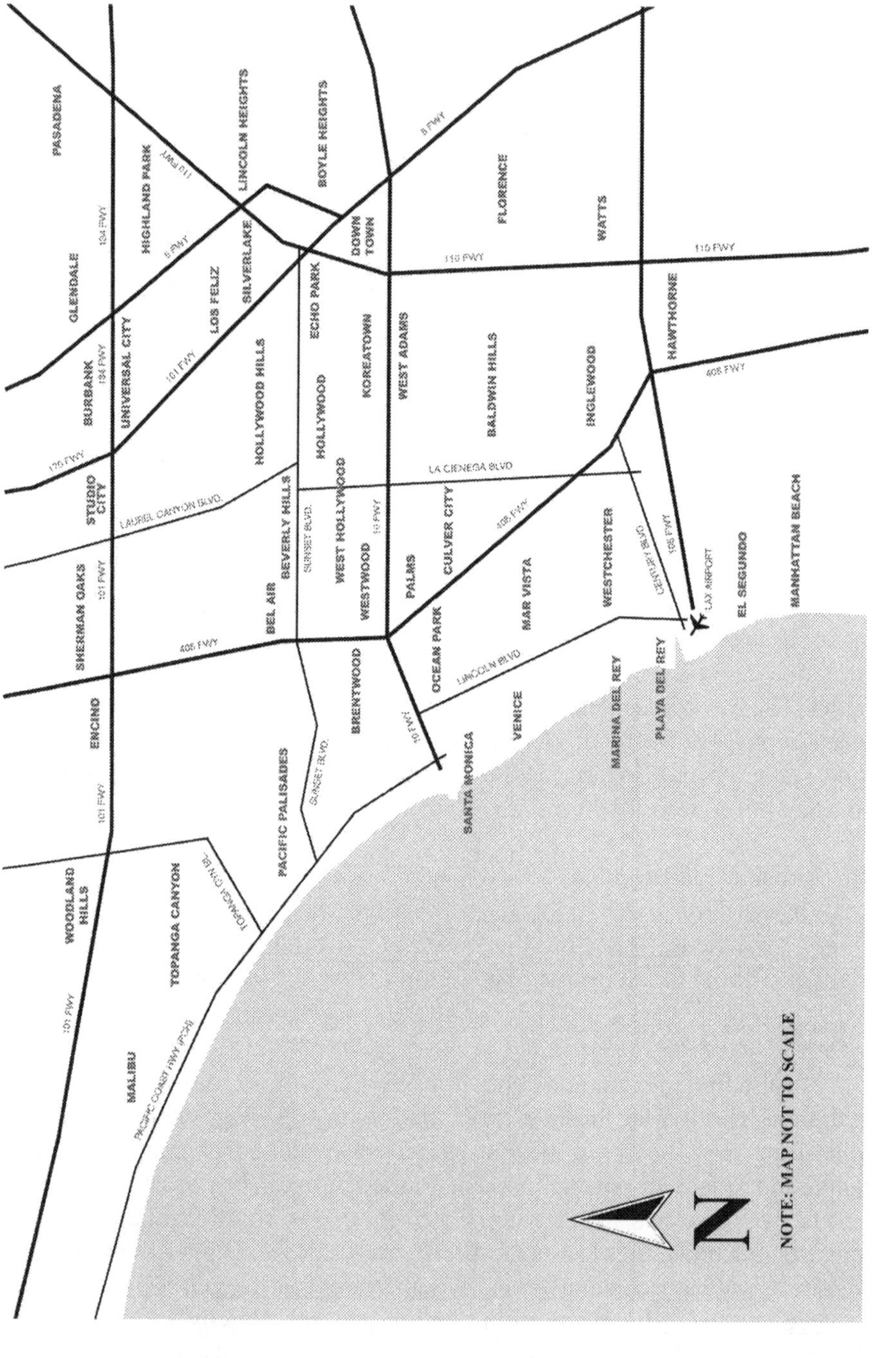
PASADENA
GLENDALE
BURBANK
STUDIO CITY
SHERMAN OAKS
ENCINO
WOODLAND HILLS
MALIBU
TOPANGA CANYON
PACIFIC PALISADES
BEL AIR
BEVERLY HILLS
HOLLYWOOD HILLS
UNIVERSAL CITY
HIGHLAND PARK
LOS FELIZ
SILVERLAKE
LINCOLN HEIGHTS
BOYLE HEIGHTS
DOWN TOWN
ECHO PARK
HOLLYWOOD
KOREATOWN
WEST HOLLYWOOD
WESTWOOD
BRENTWOOD
SANTA MONICA
VENICE
OCEAN PARK
PALMS
CULVER CITY
WEST ADAMS
BALDWIN HILLS
FLORENCE
WATTS
INGLEWOOD
HAWTHORNE
MAR VISTA
WESTCHESTER
MARINA DEL REY
PLAYA DEL REY
LAX AIRPORT
EL SEGUNDO
MANHATTAN BEACH
101 FWY
134 FWY
170 FWY
405 FWY
5 FWY
110 FWY
10 FWY
105 FWY
LAUREL CANYON BLVD.
LA CIENEGA BLVD
SUNSET BLVD.
LINCOLN BLVD
CENTURY BLVD
PACIFIC COAST HWY (PCH)
N
NOTE: MAP NOT TO SCALE

List of difficult Los Angeles street names, abbreviations, neighborhoods, and their common vernacular pronunciation:

STREET NAME	PHONETIC PRONUNCIATION
Alvarado	**AL'**-vuh-**Rawh'**-doh
Buena Vista	**BWAY'**-nuh **VISS'**-tuh
Cahuenga	kuh-**WENG'**-uh
Cañon (Beverly Hills)	**KANN'**-uhn
Centinela	**SEN'**-teh-**Nell'**-uh
Chautaugua	shuh-**TAH'**-kwah
Doheny	doe-**HEE'**-nee
Duquesne	doo-**KAYN'**
Figueroa	**FIG'**-err-**Oh'**-uh
Kanan Dume	**KAYN'**-enn **DOOM'**
La Brea	**LUH' BRAY'**-uh
La Cienega	**LAH'** see-**ENN'**-ih-guh
La Tijera	**LAH'** tee-**HAYR'**-uh
Las Virgenes	**LOSS' VERR'**-juh-ness
Los Feliz	**LOESS' FEE'**-liz
Mulholland	mull-**HALL'**-und
Pico	**PEE'**-koh
Rodeo (Baldwin Hills)	**ROE'**-dee-oh
Rodeo (Beverly Hills)	roe-**DAY'**-oh
San Vicente	**SANN'** vih-**SENN'**-tay
Sepulveda	seh-**PUHL'**-vuh-duh
Temescal	teh-**MESS'**-kull
Topanga	tuh-**PANG'**-uh
Tujunga	tuh-**HUNG'**-uh
Ventura	ven-**TOUR'**-ah; ven-**CHURR'**-ah
Wilshire	**WILL'**-shurr

PCH: Pacific Coast Highway
Cyn.: Canyon

CITY NAME	**PHONETIC PRONUNCIATION**
Agoura Hills	ah-**GOO'**-ruh **HILLS'**
Calabasas	**Cal'**-eh-**BASS'**-uss
Camarillo	**Cam'**-ah-**REE'**-oh
Castaic	cas-**TAY'**-ick
El Segundo	**ELL'** se-**GOON'**-doh
La Cañada	**LAH'** kan-**YAH'**-duh
La Crescenta	**LAH'** kreh-**SEN'**-tuh
Los Feliz	**LOESS' FEE'**-liz
Pacoima	pah-**KOY'**-mah
Tujunga	tuh-**HUNG'**-uh
Van Nuys	**VANN' NIZE'**

A word on Los Angeles-area neighborhoods: just because a neighborhood is central, convenient, expensive or clean-looking does NOT mean that it is safe. Do not be misled by bars on the windows—many homes in very fine neighborhoods have them. When assessing a neighborhood, look for obvious red flags: excessive graffiti, heavy police presence, broken-down junked cars parked on the streets, overabundance of above-ground telephone poles & wires, stray dogs, large homeless contingent, lack of foliage. I know it sounds ridiculous, but, with the exception of Downtown LA historic district, most good, safe neighborhoods have lots of healthy foliage. A general lack of foliage = dodgy neighborhood. To really test an area, drive through it at night. See who is hanging around, how noisy it is, how much activity is going on, what the parking situation is like, and see how safe you feel.

There is a book by the name of ZANY's Neighborhood Guide to Los Angeles that you might find helpful in your quest. This book is available on www.amazon.com, and it details the entire makeup of any given neighborhood in Los Angeles, including statistics on average age, income, education level, sample rent prices, and so on. Armed with your apartment listings and neighborhood breakdowns, it is time to hit the road and get looking.

The housing market in Los Angeles fluctuates greatly—at some times of the year, it is a landlord's market, and at other times, it is a tenant's market. These seasons vary, but summer is usually a very busy time in the rental market. When you go to see an apartment, you would be well-advised to have two forms of picture ID, a recent paycheck stub, and your checkbook with you. If you love the apartment and there are already five people there to see it, you may be the one who ends up getting it because you are the only one there who is fully prepared to rent it. When signing a lease, you should expect to pay first month's rent, last (final) month's rent, and a security deposit.

Ten things to ask when looking at an apartment in Los Angeles: 1) How long is the lease?, 2) Can I have a pet?, 3) Is parking included? (this is not always a given), 4) Is there a laundry facility on the premises?, 5) Can I paint/make improvements?, 6) How far away is it from the hospital, police station, freeway, my job, 7-11, schools—whatever is important to you, 7) What utilities are included?, 8) What appliances are included?, 9) How soon can I move in?, 10) How did it do in the last earthquake? The earthquake concerns are real here in Los Angeles. The big quake (a 6.8 temblor in January, 1994) took out buildings in Northridge, Granada Hills, Sherman Oaks, Mid-City, AND Santa Monica. No two earthquakes produce the same results, but when renting a place, it is good to know how well it fared in the '94 quake.

Once you have found a place you like, make sure that all of the improvements promised to you by management (new paint, new carpet, appliances, whatever) are done before you move in. Additionally, it is a good idea to get a Renter's Insurance Policy from a reputable insurance company. In the case of a catastrophe (like an earthquake) your possessions will be covered.

To protect your privacy, you may want to set up a Post Office Box at a Post Office in your neighborhood. No matter how many times you move, you can always keep the PO Box as a permanent address. It is also considered a business expense, and therefore a write-off at tax time.

In the absence of immediate job possibilities, you may want to register with a temporary placement agency to get you started. There are many temp agencies in Los Angeles that provide placements to the entertainment industry, as well as other corporate and/or industrial businesses. The following is a list of reputable temp agencies in Los Angeles:

1) The Career Group
   Century City: 10100 Santa Monica Blvd., #900
   310/277-8188

2) Apple One—several branch locations, including:
   Westwood: 1250 Westwood Blvd.
   310/477-0021

Culver City: 3812 Main St.
310/839-2450
Los Angeles: 11444 W. Olympic Bl., #260
310/445-4111
Sherman Oaks: 15165 Ventura Bl., #120
818/995-1130
Los Angeles: 888 S. Figueroa #170
213/892-0234
Santa Monica: 2629 Wilshire Blvd.
310/828-6622

3) Friedman Personnel Agency
Hollywood: 9000 W. Sunset Blvd. #1000
310/550-1002

4) Our Gang Agency
Los Angeles: 1417 Belfast Dr.
323/653-4381

5) Comar Agency
Beverly Hills: 9615 Brighton Way
310/248-2700

The advantage to registering with several agencies is that you will work more often. Agency A may not have any placements right away, but Agency E may have a two-week assignment available immediately.

When you register with the agency, they will ask you to take a grammar, spelling, typing, computer skills, and basic math test. It doesn't matter where you went to college or how many degrees you have, you will be required to take these tests. If you have specific placement requests (including salary, location, skill set, hours, days per week), make sure that the agency knows about them straight away. If your interest is to be placed in an entertainment setting, tell them. Many temp agencies also place candidates in temp-to-perm situations. If an agency is trying to fill a permanent placement at William Morris Agency, and you have the option of temp-to-perm with them (and your interests lie with representation) it's a match made in Heaven. Be straightforward with your placement representative.

There are other temporary job opportunities available that do not involve an office environment, including catering, au pair or nanny work, and waiting tables. These opportunities can be found in the newspaper, by word-of-mouth, or, in the case of au pair work, through an agency like Buckingham Nannies www.buckinghamnannies.com.

If you have a job interview in the entertainment industry during your Scout, you may wonder what to wear. With a job interview in the corporate world, there is never a question: you wear a suit, and you look polished. In the entertainment field, this is not the case. If you are going for a meeting/interview at a top-shelf talent agency (William Morris Agency, Creative Artists Agency, International Creative Management) or at a major studio (Sony, Walt Disney Studios, Universal, Paramount) for a job that requires desk work (assistant or associate work) then yes, you can wear a suit or a very sharp upscale outfit. If you are going in for an interview for a production job (Production Assistant, Intern, General Assistant) the look is casual. Specifically, that means something like khaki pants or very nice jeans and a sweater or clean shirt—a *GAP* or *Banana Republic*-type look. You should look put-together, not sloppy, but it would be an embarrassing and unforgettable mistake to show up in a suit.

MOVING TRUCKS AND GETTING SETTLED

So you've moved your things in, set up what you can, and now you need to make a supplies run. For the bigger items, your tastes and aesthetic sensibilities will determine where you will spend your cash; your options are virtually unlimited in this city. For the basics, however, the following list of move-in stores and their locations will help:

TARGET (Bicycles, brooms, birthday cards, boom boxes and everything else)
- — Hollywood
  7100 Santa Monica Blvd (at La Brea) 323/603-0005
- — Culver City
  10820 Jefferson Blvd. 310/839-5200
- — Sherman Oaks
  5711 Sepulveda Blvd. 818/779-0163
- — Van Nuys
  14920 Raymer St. 818/922-1001
- — North Hollywood
  11051 Victory Blvd. 818/761-3083
- — Burbank
  1800 Empire Ave. 818/238-0132

K-MART (Inexpensive linens, appliances, housewares, sundry items)
— West Hollywood
6310 W. 3rd St. 323/933-7306
— Burbank
1000 N. San Fernando Blvd. 818/843-4221
— North Hollywood
13007 Sherman Way 818/764-0250
— Los Angeles
3150 N. San Fernando Rd. 323/257-8261
— Los Angeles
5850 S. Vermont Ave. 323/753-1464

HOME DEPOT (Home-related building, garden, and maintenance supplies)
— Hollywood
5600 W. Sunset Blvd. 323/461-3303
— Downtown Los Angeles
1675 Wilshire Blvd. 213/273-8464
— South Los Angeles
4925 W. Slauson Ave. 323/298-4610
— Glendale
5040 San Fernando Rd. 818/246-9600
— North Hollywood
11600 Sherman Way 818/759-5421

BED, BATH & BEYOND (Accessories for the kitchen, bath, and bedroom)
— Los Angeles—Beverly Center
142 S. San Vicente Blvd. 310/652-1380
— Hollywood
1557 Vine St. (at Sunset Blvd.) 323/460-4500
— Studio City
12555 Ventura Blvd. 818/980-0260
— West Los Angeles
11801 W. Olympic Blvd. 310/478-5767

IKEA (Swedish-designed furniture at reasonable prices)
— Burbank
600 N. San Fernando Rd. 818/842-4532
— Carson
20700 Avalon Blvd. #910 310/527-4532
— City of Industry
17621 Gale Ave. 626/912-4532

STAPLES (Office, business, and computer supplies & electronics)
- — Hollywood
  6450 W. Sunset Blvd. 323/467-2155
- — Los Angeles
  5407 Wilshire Blvd. 323/965-5240
- — Los Angeles
  1839 S. La Cienega Blvd. 310/202-5343
- — Studio City
  12605 Ventura Blvd. 818/753-6390
- — Burbank
  1060 W. Alameda 818/558-3350

Other things you will probably be looking for:

GENTLY USED FURNITURE
- — Just Like the Model
  18429 Pacific St., Fountain Valley 714/968-9888
- — Eclectic Avenue
  2516 Overland Ave. Culver City 310/837-2626
  2307 Main St., Santa Monica 310/392-3390

ANTIQUE STORES
- — Wertz Brothers Furniture: West Los Angeles
  11879 Santa Monica Blvd. 310/477-4251
- — Wertz Brothers Antique Mart: Santa Monica
  1607 Lincoln Blvd. 310/452-1800
- — Antique Guild: Mid-City
  3225 Helms Ave. 310/559-1114
- — Antique Mall: Sherman Oaks
  14034 Ventura Blvd. 818/906-0338
- — Antique Center: Culver City
  5431 Sepulveda Blvd. 310/391-1996

THRIFT STORES
- — Goodwill 888/446-6394 *Many locations, including*
  West Los Angeles: 11726 Santa Monica Blvd @ Stoner
  Hollywood: 1200 Vine @ Lexington
  North Hollywood: 5855 Lankershim Blvd.
- — Out of the Closet *Many locations, including*
  West Los Angeles: 1608 Sawtelle Blvd. 310/473-7787

Hollywood: 6210 Sunset Blvd. 323/467-6811
West Hollywood: 8224 Santa Monica Blvd. 323/848-9760
— Salvation Army *Many locations, including*
Santa Monica: 1658 11th St. 310/581-7987
Culver City: 11160 Washington Blvd. 310/836-8344
North Hollywood: 6120 Lankershim Blvd. 818/985-8105
— St. Vincent de Paul
Atwater Village: 210 North Avenue 21 323/221-6191

DEPARTMENT OF MOTOR VEHICLES: 1-800-777-0133
— Hollywood
803 N. Cole Ave.
— Culver City
11400 Washington Blvd.
— Santa Monica
2235 Colorado Ave.
— Burbank
1866 Hollywood Way
1335 W. Glenoaks Ave.

WALK-IN MEDICAL CLINICS: No appointment necessary (can save you hundreds of dollars in comparison to the emergency room)

— Los Angeles Free Clinic
8405 Beverly Blvd. (at Orlando)
Los Angeles 90048 TEL: 323/653-8622
Offers free, or minimal cost health and dental care

— Tarzana Treatment Center
18646 Oxnard St.
Tarzana 91356 TEL: 818/996-1051
Offers free, or minimal cost health and dental care

— Venice Family Clinic
604 Rose Ave.,
Venice 90291 TEL: 310/392-8630, ext. 210
Offers free, or minimal cost health and dental care

Getting from place to place in your new city may prove to be a bit frustrating with traffic and freeway confusion. A must-have for every Los Angeles newbie is the THOMAS GUIDE, a page-by-page street map book of the Los Angeles area. They can be purchased at any local bookstore, and at most 7-11 locations. You will never be sorry that you have a Thomas Guide, and you will use it every day, guaranteed. For traffic updates, there are two local AM radio stations that give reports every ten minutes or so. They are KNX 1070 and KFWB 980. Their reports can save you a lot of time if you check in advance of your departure.

A final checklist of the move-in duties:

- Transfer all prescriptions to a pharmacy near your new home
- Open a bank account
- Get a California Driver's License
- Register your car in California
- Get new automobile insurance
- Sign up with Southern California Automobile Association (known as AAA elsewhere)
- Transfer your health insurance to a local branch or carrier
- Get renter's insurance
- Complete all change of address forms through the Post Office

A checklist of move-in concerns for which you may want a referral:

- Medical doctor
- Dentist
- Hair stylist/manicurist/waxer
- Accountant
- Therapist
- Internet Service Provider
- Cellular phone service
- Auto mechanic

The most physical adjustment you will likely make is to the weather. It is almost always a beautiful day here in Los Angeles. There is virtually no Fall or Winter here—there is only Spring, Summer, Cooler Summer, and Cold Summer. The rainy season is from January to April, and rarely, if ever, does the lowest of low temperatures get below 45° F. July, August and September can be quite warm, with many days over 100° F, lows in the 60° F range at the lowest. With this in mind, you may need to adjust your wardrobe, or plan accordingly. If you are planning on working in production, do not jump to throw away all of your winter clothes. You may need those warm sweaters and jackets on night exterior locations, when you are outside in the 45° F temperatures for 16 hours straight.

HANGING OUT IN THE KNOW

Once you get your place settled, you will probably need something to eat and a cool beverage. Maybe even a spa treatment. Where to go? The possibilities are endless. You can combine your eating, drinking, and relaxing with schmoozing and job-searching if you like. There are many spots in town that are legendary for deal-making—famous hotspots that you might want to investigate as part of your Los Angeles indoctrination. The following list includes spots for breakfast, lunch, and dinner, major mall locations, as well as some of the best spas in Los Angeles—some of these places are perched on the back door of major studios. That means you can sniff around and find out who's making deals with whom.

Eateries/Watering Holes	*Address*	*Telephone*	*Neighborhood*	*Best Time to Go*
AOC	8022 W 3rd St	323/ 653-6359	Los Angeles	Dinner
Bar Marmont	8171 W Sunset Blvd	323/ 650-0575	West Hollywood	Weekday Nights
Barney Greengrass	9570 Wilshire Blvd	310/ 777-5877	Beverly Hills	Lunch
Casa Vega	13301 Ventura Blvd	818/ 788-4868	Sherman Oaks	Dinner/Drinks
Chan Dara	310 N Larchmont Blvd	323/ 467-1052	Los Angeles	Dinner/Drinks
Chaya Brasserie	8741 Alden Dr	310/ 859-8833	Los Angeles	Dinner/Drinks
Chin Chin Sunset Plaza	8618 W Sunset Blvd	310/ 652-1818	West Hollywood	Lunch
Cravings Sunset Plaza	8653 W Sunset Blvd	310/ 652-6103	West Hollywood	Lunch
Crustacean	9646 Santa Monica Blvd	310/ 205-8990	Beverly Hills	Dinner/Drinks
Dalt's Grill	3500 W Olive Ave # 100	818/ 953-7750	Burbank	Lunch
Delfini at Fred Segal	500 Broadway	310/ 395-5699	Santa Monica	Lunch
Dimples	3413 W Olive Ave	818/ 842-2336	Burbank	Drinks/all nights
Four Seasons Bar	300 S Doheny Dr	310/ 273-2222	Beverly Hills	Drinks/all nights
Grace	7360 Beverly Blvd	323/ 934-4400	Los Angeles	Dinner
Hugo's	8401 Santa Monica Blvd	323/ 654-3993	West Hollywood	Breakfast/Brunch
Il Cielo	9018 Burton Way	310/ 276-9990	Beverly Hills	Dinner
Ivy	113 N Robertson Blvd	310/ 274-8303	Los Angeles	Lunch
Jerry's Deli Beverly	8701 Beverly Blvd	310/ 289-1811	West Hollywood	Lunch/Dinner
Jerry's Deli Studio City	12655 Ventura Blvd	818/ 980-4245	Studio City	Lunch/Dinner
Kate Mantilini	9101 Wilshire Blvd	310/ 278-3699	Beverly Hills	Lunch
Koi	730 N La Cienega Blvd	310/ 659-9449	West Hollywood	Dinner
Lucques	8474 Melrose Ave	323/ 655-6277	Los Angeles	Dinner
Manhattan Won Ton Co.	151 S Doheny Dr	310/ 888-2804	Beverly Hills	Lunch
Mauro's Café at Fred Segal	8100 Melrose Ave	323/ 653-2874	Los Angeles	Lunch
Morton's	8764 Melrose Ave	310/ 276-5205	West Hollywood	Monday nights
Mr. Chow	344 N. Camden	310/ 278-9911	Beverly Hills	Dinner
Musso & Frank's	6667 Hollywood Blvd	323/ 467-7788	Hollywood	Dinner
Newsroom	120 N Robertson Blvd	310/ 652-4444	West Hollywood	Breakfast/Lunch
Peninsula Hotel	9882 Santa Monica Blvd	310/ 551-2888	Beverly Hills	Breakfast
Pink's Hot Dogs	709 N La Brea	323/ 931-4223	Los Angeles	Lunch/Dinner
Roscoe's Chicken & Waffles	1514 N Gower St	323/ 466-7453	Hollywood	Lunch/Dinner
Saddle Ranch	8371 W Sunset Blvd	323/ 822-3850	West Hollywood	Weekday Nights
Spago	176 N Canon Dr	310/ 385-0880	Beverly Hills	Weekday Nights
Spanish Kitchen	826 N La Cienega Blvd	310/ 659-4794	West Hollywood	Dinner
Sushi Roku	8445 W 3rd St	323/ 655-6767	West Hollywood	Dinner
Swingers	8020 Beverly Blvd	323/ 653-5858	Los Angeles	Late-night
The Farm of Beverly Hills	439 N Beverly Dr	323/ 525-1699	Beverly Hills	Lunch
The Sky Bar at Mondrian	8440 W Sunset Blvd	323/ 848-6025	West Hollywood	Weekday Nights
The Standard Downtown	550 S Flower St	213/ 892-8080	Downtown	Weekday Nights
The Standard Hotel/Bar	8300 W Sunset Blvd	323/ 650-9090	West Hollywood	Weekday Nights
Toast	8221 W 3rd St	323/ 655-5018	West Hollywood	Lunch
Urth Caffé	8565 Melrose Ave	310/ 659-0628	West Hollywood	Lunch/coffee

Shopping Meccas

American Rag	150 S La Brea Ave	323/ 935-3154	Los Angeles
Century City Shopping Center	10250 Santa Monica Blvd	310/ 553-5300	Century City
Fred Segal	8100 Melrose Ave	323/ 651-4129	Los Angeles
The Beverly Center	8500 Beverly Blvd	310/ 854-0070	West Hollywood
The Grove	189 The Grove Dr	323/ 900-8000	Los Angeles

Salon/Spa

Anastacia Salon	438 N Bedford Dr	310/ 273-3155	Beverly Hills
Burke Williams Day Spa	8000 W Sunset Blvd # 130	323/ 822-9007	West Hollywood
John Frieda Salon	8440 Melrose Pl	323/ 653-4040	West Hollywood
Jose Eber Salon	224 N Rodeo Dr	310/ 278-7646	Beverly Hills
Kinara Spa	656 N Robertson Blvd	310/ 657-9188	West Hollywood
Ole Henriksen Spa	8622 A W Sunset Blvd	310/ 854-7700	West Hollywood

Welcome to Los Angeles. You have just completed the first step in "going Hollywood". It gets better from here!

INTERVIEW

Subject: Claire Best
C.O.O. & Agent, Sandra Marsh Management

Hometown: Sevenoaks, Kent, UK
Moved to LA: 1991

Topic: Going With the Flow of Life in LA

Where did you go/what did you study in college (university)?

I went to Durham University in the North of England. I graduated with a B.A. Honours Degree in French & Spanish with subsidiary Portuguese.

How did you decide to move to Los Angeles?

It happened by accident. I had finished working on a drama documentary in Japan and had some friends who were working out here on another documentary in L.A.. They suggested that I take a break in the sun and come out to L.A. and hang out with them while they filmed. I arrived just a few days after the riots in May, 1991. After a couple of weeks here, another documentary came up for me about the legendary director Sam Peckinpah for the BBC. Since the film was going to require a fair amount of research in Los Angeles, I looked into finding an apartment to live in for the summer. I struck lucky and ended up living in a gorgeous house above Lake Hollywood which I found on the Screen Actors Guild noticeboard as a sublet with two roommates: two gay guys who became like my brothers over the years. I started to feel very at home in Los Angeles and went to buy my first car: a Volkswagen convertible Beetle. I remember the first day I got it, putting down the hood and driving forever along the top of Mulholland. It was terrific! When my research was done, I set up the shooting portion of the documentary and we interviewed a lot of people that Sam Peckinpah had known in Los Angeles. Then it seemed to make sense for me to stay on in L.A. and to handle the U.S. end of all the other projects for the London production company I been working with.

Did you have family or friends to help you or support you in your move?

Not really—my father went to school with the director Ken Russell and thought that anyone connected to the film industry was eccentric…I only had one connection here which was a friend of my documentary pals.

What was the hardest adjustment?

It's a long way from home and the time difference is hard. Just when you are full of energy in the morning, everyone in England is tired of the day and ready to go to bed. Also, it is hard to be in a city where everyone who is here has really come for career reasons and not family reasons—it can make the place seem peculiarly unemotional for a while until you get a network of friends around you. I always say that L.A. is an airport that somehow became a city (everyone in the industry at least, comes here on their way to or from somewhere (Australia, New Zealand, Hong Kong, Japan, Europe….) and somehow they stay, as this is where Mecca is for the entertainment industry.

What was your first job in Los Angeles, and how did you get it?

For a while I ran the Los Angeles end of a London based documentary company, Lucida Productions. I was able to get my work visa by proving that I brought a certain amount of employment to America with the documentaries that I was producing. I then had a while when I was script supervising in between producing documentaries. I worked with Paul Bartel on his last film *Shelf Life* and with Whit Stillman on *Barcelona*. I loved script supervising as it is probably the best position on the set to really understand how a movie is made, how a director works, how a D.P. (*Director of Photography*) works, how a script works, what scenes you can live without if you need to etc., etc. As a script supervisor you are responsible for providing an accurate log of what has been filmed to the editor so you learn what is important for that, too. I had always wanted to transition into features when I was in England and I used the script supervising as a way to do that. It is an incredibly useful background to have.

How did you decide on representation as a career?

One of the documentaries that I produced *Naked Making Lunch*—about William Burroughs and David Cronenberg and the whole concept of filming the unfilmable in literature—received a very good review in *Variety* and resulted in a lot of meetings for the director, Chris Rodley. I persuaded Chris that he should use this interest to go out and do a short dramatic film which I would produce. We raised the money and made the short.

From that I then went on to produce another short for Disney and then to produce a film for the Artist/Photographer, William Wegman: *The Hardly Boys in Hardly Gold*, featuring all dogs. One of the executives I worked with at Disney went on to work at New Line and asked me if I would help out on a freelance assignment there to review a board and budget. One thing lead to another and I ended up going on staff at New Line as a physical production executive for 5 years. I never really had any intention to stay there that long, as I had wanted to get back into producing and had a number of feature scripts that were in various stages of packaging. But I learnt there that being an independent producer and supporting yourself is an impossible task for all but a handful.

I had always had a close association with Sandra Marsh. When I first came to L.A. for the documentary research, I met her and it was Sandra who introduced me to Disney. Over the years I would recommend clients to her and we formed a close friendship. In 2001, my boss at New Line was forced to leave due to illness and I knew that it was time to move on. Sandra approached me and asked if I would consider joining her in helping her to run the agency. She wanted someone who had a producing and studio background, and it just seemed like the perfect fit. It was a risky career change for me, but I am thrilled that I made it and never look back.

At the end of the day, matchmaking talent is what I am best at and being an agent in a small management/agency company allows you to do that. It is very exciting to introduce a director to a new creative talent that they have not come across before. It is also great to be part of a small company. The experience of a large corporation is great but ultimately you are just a cog in the wheel. In a small company you work harder but the satisfaction is much greater.

What things do you like about Los Angeles?

Like all Brits, the weather! I love the fact that this is a first class city yet everywhere there are open spaces, trees, mountains and the beach. You don't feel like you have to escape the city to the countryside at the weekends—you can see the countryside everyday.

How long did it take for Los Angeles to feel like your home?

Four years. Initially I settled in very quickly but it takes about that long for friends to stick and for you to establish yourself in the industry.

Anything you would have done differently?

No—there will always be films that I would have liked to have finished developing to produce but I have managed to executive produce a couple of independent features (*Cleopatra's Second Husband* and *50 Ways to Leave Your Lover*).

Anything else you'd like to add?

I married an American (writer/director Jordan Hawley) whom I met here and we have 2 children (Lara 3, Juliette 1).

CHAPTER THREE

WORK

Some people come to Los Angeles with very specific career paths and goals in mind. Consider yourself lucky if you are one of those people right out of the gates. In order to be successful in the entertainment industry, you will need to *become* a person with very specific career path ideas and goals in mind. There are transitional steps involved in attaining these goals, but it helps to know where to point the gun. That way, when you start pulling the trigger, you have a chance of hitting the target.

In the Appendix section of this book, there is a thorough table of job listings and their descriptions.*(P.165)* Review it carefully, and see what suits your personality and interests.

If you are still trying to figure out what you would like to do, set a target date for making a decision about your career plans. Give yourself some time to try different avenues of entertainment, and then see which area suits your personality and your skills most appropriately. You may give yourself three months, six months, or a year to make these decisions, but set a deadline. The longer you drag your heels about which direction to take, the harder it is to make a decision. Hollywood moves quickly, and so should you. Seize your opportunities.

If you arrive in Los Angeles with no job, and need to make money quickly to get on your feet, the easiest solution is temping. In chapter two, there are five agencies listed that place candidates in entertainment settings. This is an ideal setup for someone interested in working in talent management, producing, development, distribution and/or marketing. The temp agency may be able to provide you entry-level work as a temporary ASSISTANT. Pay very careful attention to the way business is done, the language used, the politics at play—you can learn valuable industry street-skills as a temp, take them to your next job, and get paid in the process. Even if you hate your temp placement, it is only temporary. You can continue your job search while you are temping, to find something suitable to your interests and personality.

Being an assistant means that you are supporting operations in any given field. There are many different types of assistants, including:

Actor's Assistant	Similar to the job description for Assistant to the Director, the Actor's Assistant usually helps to make life and work run smoothly for their employer. This position requires close contact with the actor's manager and agents, as the assistant will be the immediate point of contact for information from, and scheduling with, the actor.
Agent's Assistant	An office-based job, this position usually requires good phone and computer skills, as well as an excellent memory. Included in duties (usually) are script-reading, client scheduling, and information gathering.
Assistant to Director	Takes care of all business that Director cannot attend to himself or herself. Often this includes making phone calls, keeping schedules, getting lunch, setting up meetings, ensuring that the director's life and work run smoothly.
Assistant to Producer	Usually more of an office job, can be very demanding and interesting. Often keeps schedule for producer, arranging meetings, screenings, logistics of anything and everything that goes on in the office.
Development Assistant	Reads scripts, writes coverage (basic description of the plot & characters), aids the executive in developing projects, gathers information pertinent to projects in development, answers phones & correspondence.
Executive Assistant	Depending on the type of executive, this is a higher-level placement similar to the Assistant to the Producer job description. Often demanding, opportunities for placement include assisting Directors of Marketing, Distribution, Post-Production, up to Presidents of studios. Not an appropriate placement for a first job; these positions require experience.
Production Company Assistant	Usually works as a gopher, doing whatever office work and/or runs (errands) need to be done.

Production Office Assistant (PA)	Photocopies scripts, crew lists, and all paperwork, answers phones, goes on runs, orders lunch for crew, serves as liaison between the set and the production office.
Writer's Assistant (other)	Depending on the type of writer, the job duties for this position may include answering phones & other correspondence, organizing schedules, printing drafts, copying scripts, and going on runs for the writer.
Writer's Assistant (TV)	This position usually is quite busy with note-taking and script-typing. A typical writer's assistant on a TV show sits in on story meetings, furiously typing away into their laptop, turning ideas into outlines so that they can be developed later by the team of writers. This position requires strong computer skills, as well as a very good grasp of language and grammar.

There are occasionally some shortcuts to getting a very good assistant job in film and television production companies, agencies, or the studio system:

1) UTA Job List
   Available to those "in the know"—you have to know someone who works at United Talent Agency to get a copy of this list, but it is the cream-of-the-crop of job opportunities for assistant and executive placements.

2) Studio Job Listings
   www.foxcareers.com (Fox Studios)
   http://disney.go.com/disneycareers/ (Disney)
   http://www.mtvncareers.com (MTV)
   http://www.turnerjobs.com (Turner Broadcasting)
   http://www.tvjobs.com (general TV job listings)
   http://www.wbjobs.com (Warner Brothers)
   http://www.employnow.com (general TV & film job listings)

3) Studio Job Hotlines
   The following are a list of job hotlines operated and maintained by some of the studios in town:

Cartoon Network	818/729-4200
E! Entertainment	323/954-2710 (internships only)
MTV, VH1, Nickelodeon	310/752-8008

New Line Cinema	310/967-6553
Paramount	323/956-5216
Sony Pictures	310/244-4436
Universal Studios	818/777-5627
Walt Disney Studios	818/558-2222
Warner Brothers	818/954-5400

4) Agent Training Program
Some agencies, like William Morris Agency, have agent training programs. In order to be considered for the WMA program, you will need to demonstrate a strong degree of computer literacy, highly developed written, verbal and inter-personal skills, possess some industry experience (paid or unpaid) and a desire to continue in the industry, and you will need to have earned a degree from a four-year accredited college or university. Meeting those qualifications, you can APPLY for the program. Those qualifications alone will not get you into the training program. It is very competitive, but well worth the time to apply if you are interested in the field.
William Morris: www.wma.com; 310/859-4000

5 DGA Trainee Program
www.trainingplan.org; 818/386-2545
Known fondly on the set as the "DGA Trainee", this lucky person is participating in the Director's Guild of America's Assistant Directors Training Program. Trainees complete 400 days of on-the-job training in film, episodic television, pilots, miniseries, and the like, while attending seminars organized by the DGA for their education. The end purpose is to turn the trainees into Second Assistant Directors, ready for the industry. Trainees are paid, though minimally, and it is competitive to get accepted into the program. Requirements for application include a degree from an accredited four-year or two-year college or university, or two years paid work experience, or E-5 or higher military discharge, and all applicants must be over 21 years of age.

6) WGA Trainee Program
www.wga.org/manuals/training.html; 323/782-4548
The Writer's Guild of America offers a training program that exists to provide opportunities to aspiring writers who happen to be women, people over 40 years of age, or physically disabled. These opportunities are for television writing, as they have the most stable,

long-lived training situation in the business. This is a situation where, if you want it, you are going to have to chase it down. It is up to YOU to contact the show in which you are interested. You will have to send the Executive Producer of the show your resume (thoroughly representing your writing background), and a well-written cover letter expressing your intentions. WGA Trainees are paid, again, minimally, but the opportunity to be a trainee is very valuable.

7) www.filmstaff.com
There are many job sites on the internet for entertainment, but one of the most substantial is www.filmstaff.com. They list literally hundreds of job opportunities for different fields in the business, including entry-level jobs like PAs, Development Assistants, Wardrobe Assistants, Assistant Production Coordinators, Assistant Editors, Runners, and Craft Service. The list is endless, and includes job listings from Animators to Special Effects to Editors to Directors. You must be a member to access the job listings; a trial 5-day membership is around $5, monthly membership is around $20, or you can join for one full year for $99.

8) www.entertainmentcareers.net
Another great wealth of job opportunities is www.entertainementcareers.net—it is a free service, and they offer up a staggering number of job listings in the following categories: acting/casting notices, advertising, agency/management, animation/graphic design, assistant and entry level, broadcast news, broadcasting/sound/music engineering, casting, commercial production, crew jobs, crew jobs (low/unpaid/deferred), executive positions, fashion, feature/TV development, feature/TV production, film festivals, human resources, internet, internships, IS/IT, legal/business affairs, marketing/promotions/PR, MBAs, multimedia/video game, music, post production, publishing, radio, sales, sports, studios, theater, theatrical exhibition & distribution, TV networks, TV stations, visual FX, and writing. The sheer number of job postings on this site is a bit overwhelming, but the companies posting those job opportunities are top-shelf and deserve a look.

9) www.ifilmpro.com
   This site is linked with Hollywood Creative Directory, and job listings are posted in categories that include: Creative (Producers, Execs, Assistants, Staff), Agents and Managers (Agents, Managers, Casting, and Casting Assistants), New Media (Web Designers), Distributors (Sales, Marketing, PR, Merchandising), Production/Post Production (Crew, Editors, FX, Graphic Artists), Support (Assistants, Personal Assistants, Receptionists, Personal Trainers, Personal Shoppers), Interns (Entertainment Industry Internships—no pay), Film Crews (Paid), Film Crews (Unpaid), and Miscellaneous (Everything else).

If you want to pursue writing, production crafts or directing, you may want a temporary placement in a line of work that provides for more flexible hours in the day (to accommodate meetings, writing and developing your own projects). Good placements in this vein include catering, part-time nanny or au pair work, bartending, or waiting tables. These positions usually provide work at night, on weekends or at odd hours, freeing up your weekdays for interviews and/or the occasional internship or free gig.

There is a huge difference between production work in film, television, music videos and commercials. If you are hired on a film as a production assistant (PA), you may be working for three months or more at a stretch. On a film, you will work either five or six days per week, and on average 13—16 hours per day. You may or may not get overtime, mileage, or cell phone reimbursement. If you are hired as an assistant in TV, you may work five to eight months at a stretch on any given show. Average daily hours vary, depending on your duties, but they can rage from 10—16 hours per day, usually five days per week. You may or may not get overtime, mileage, or cell phone reimbursement. If you are hired as a PA on a music video or commercial, you may work for one to twelve days at a stretch, five or six-day weeks. Your average hours will be 14—20 hours per day (yes, the difference is that great), but you will almost always have big fat juicy overtime to make up for it. Mileage and cell phone reimbursement will depend on the job parameters. Most production jobs will provide you with breakfast and another meal six hours after call during shooting. If the shooting day runs over thirteen hours, you will be provided at that time with what is called "second meal", usually sandwiches or fast food. In pre-production, you will be responsible for buying your own meals.

Don't be in a hurry to get on a huge movie. You can make mistakes earlier in your career that are more easily forgiven on a smaller budgeted feature. Falling on your face on a 50-million-dollar film can involve a very difficult recovery.

If you are looking for an internship or entry-level job in film production, there are a number of sources where you can find films in production, pre-production, preparation and development. They are as follows:

1) Hollywood Reporter TUESDAY EDITION
   Available at newsstands or for subscribers on line:
   www.hollywoodreporter.com

2) Daily Variety FRIDAY EDITION
   Available at newsstands or for subscribers on line:
   www.variety.com

3) Production Weekly (comes out every Thursday)
   Available online or hard copies for a fee:
   www.productionweekly.com

4) Below the Line News
   Monthly publication about artists in the *below the line* categories in filmmaking; has extensive production table for both film and television.
   www.btlnews.com

5) www.ifilmpro.com
   Their job listings page (detailed above) is linked to the Hollywood Creative Directory, listing job opportunities in film production for both paying and non-paying placements.

If you are looking to find an entry-level job in television production, you will need to start in the production office. Most television shows are unionized, which prevents a non-union employee's hands-on involvement with the actual physical production of the show. You may be allowed to work as an office production assistant, writer's assistant, and so forth, but without a union card, your production opportunities will be limited.

If you want to pursue television work on an existing program, you will need to contact the show through its production company. The two trade magazines list shows in production with production company and contact information once a week: the Daily Variety THURSDAY edition (www.dailyvariety.com), and the Hollywood Reporter on the 1st and 3rd Tuesdays of the month (www.hollywoodreporter.com). Below the Line also lists all shows monthly in their publication (www.btlnews.com). If you are unable to find the show you are looking for in those production reports, you may need to find the production office through the network that airs the show. The following is a list of some of the networks and their phone numbers:

1)	ABC, ABC Family	818/560-1000
2)	CBS Television	323/575-2345
3)	Columbia/TriStar TV	310/244-4000
4)	Disney Channel	818/569-7500
5)	FOX	310/369-1000
6)	HBO	310/201-9200
7)	MTV	310/752-8000
8)	NBC Television	818/840-4444
9)	Nickelodeon	818/736-3000
10)	Paramount	323/956-5000
11)	Showtime	310/234-5200
12)	Viacom	310/234-5000
13)	WB Television	818/954-6000

If you would like to work in music videos and/or commercials, there is a sourcebook for production companies, producers, directors, craftspeople and vendors. This book is called LA 411, and it is available at its eponymous website, www.LA411.com. It is an incredible resource, and well worth the purchase price if this is something that interests you.

A FABULOUS RESUME

In order to get a job in the entertainment industry, you will need a good solid resume. Resumes for the entertainment industry look different from resumes for the corporate world. You will need to include specific information about your background and prior work in your field. It is important that your resume be clear, organized, and easy to read. This is not a place for curlicue font or teddy bears and roses stationery. Do not lie, falsely embellish or fabricate projects on your resume. Use only what you have done, representing it accurately. You can always pad the project descriptions and list references to fill the page, but most savvy employers can see right through a made-up resume. Following are some resumes that are good examples for different fields. Let's first consider Martin Farnsworth, who is looking for work as an assistant, hopefully in development:

MARTIN FARNSWORTH

EXPERIENCE:

2004 **Red Wing Productions** Development Assistant
Director of Development: Jan Sheedy
Actively developed the horror film PuckFace, which premiered at the Slamdance Film Festival 2004.

2003 **Au Courant Management** Intern
Kitty Goliath and Vera Ferucci, Managers
Assisted managing clients, including Barbara Standish, Ched Digman, Zooey Freshinet, and Jake Gardiner.

2002 Keepin' Alive (reality series) Intern
Cayenne Productions, LLC.
Producer: Harry Ringlet; UPM: Cindy McIntosh
Helped coordinate game ideas for this hour-long multiple-camera reality show about fasting.

2001 **ABF Interiors** **Raleigh, NC** Assistant
Owner: Anna B. Fanker
Answered phones, coordinated all correspondence and scheduling for this booming interior design firm.

1999–2002 **Jo-Jo Video-a-Go-Go** **Ames, IA** Rental Clerk
Restocked videos and DVDs for consumer rental. Worked the cash register and LYNUX computer system for inventory.

EDUCATION:

University of Iowa, Ames, Iowa
Bachelor of Arts, English 2002 Dean's List

Raleigh Community College, Raleigh, North Carolina
Associate of Arts Degree, English 1999

OTHER:

President: Sigma Alpha Epsilon, Tau Chapter 2001–2002
Awards: Jay D. Simmons Award for Excellence in Writing, 2000, for essay "Withers", awarded by faculty at University of Iowa.

Martin's resume is clean-looking and well organized, good traits for someone who needs to help run an office efficiently. Let's look at his work experience. He is certainly well-diversified. He has listed all of his job experience, no matter how diverse. His time with Red Wing Productions in development tells us he has experience in the field. His time at Au Courant Management tells us that he has experience dealing with people. His experience with the reality show *Keepin' Alive* tells us that he's been in the production environment, and has seen how it works. His listing of the ABF interior design job shows that he can handle a busy office. His clerk job at the video store indicates his familiarity with films. Further, Martin's resume tells us that he has a writing background (his English major, and essay award in college) which is integral in the development area of the business. The fact that he listed his tenure as chapter president of his fraternity is significant—it shows that he has leadership skills and can handle responsibility. Martin is a great candidate for a development assistant job (or any assistant job, for that matter), and has an outstanding resume.

Shelly S. Bobelli

345 Redondo Avenue, Los Angeles, CA 90027: 323/555-8402 home; 323/555-4092 cell

EXPERIENCE:

2004 MANHUNTER, (*feature film*) Production Office Runner
Producer: Bill Banana; UPM: Julie Fanguli; POC: Barbi Dodson

2003 Paw Dar Jaunt Production Company Office Production Assistant
President: Karen Bigpants

2003 Reptile Hospital (series, Animal Planet) Intern
Writer/Producer: Kevin Snaykun; Producer: Karen Bigpants

2002 Resident Advisor Coordinator, Denison University
Responsible for all 34 Resident Assistants in the West Campus, covering over 500 students total. Conducted weekly staff meetings, oversaw entire running of student housing in my section, including orientation, disciplinary action and move-ins/move-outs.

2001 Residential Advisor, Clomberg Hall, Denison University
Responsible for 24 freshman students from new student week orientation to move-out. Served as a liaison to student affairs with any resident concerns, and handled all manner of issues from homesickness to academic probation.

1998 Summer Camp Counselor, Camp Okawocka, Wooster, Ohio
Responsible for 12 campers, ages 10–13 at this camp for at-risk youth. Supervised living arrangements and all activities with the campers for 14 days.

EDUCATION:

Denison University, Granville, Ohio
Bachelor of Arts, Art History, 2002 GPA: 3.25

Institute of Practical Arts and Sculpture, Florence, Italy
Summer Program, certification 2000

OTHER:

Free Arts for Abused Kids: Volunteer in Art Instruction 2002–present
Foreign languages: Italian, proficient; some Spanish
Computer programs known: Microsoft Office, all programs; Adobe Photoshop

References available on request

Shelli Bobelli's resume is very interesting. She's applying for a PA position on a feature film. Shelli is a recent graduate of college, but it appears she hasn't wasted her time. She lists all of her jobs, with the year only. This is not uncommon in the film industry. People are not hung up on specific dates, not even months. If you put years only, that will suffice.

Shelli has listed the major players in her employment, which is smart. You never know who is going to read your resume, and who they are going to know. If Shelli had a good relationship with the people she listed, and a potential interviewer knows that person, they can make a quick phone call to check on Shelli's character and work ethic. It's a good thing that Shelli listed people who loved working with her.

It looks like, through her work at *Reptile Hospital*, she met Karen Bigpants, who (after the show ended) hired her to work at Paw Dar Jaunt Production Company. Since Paw Dar Jaunt Production Company is Karen Bigpants' company, we can gather that she *really* liked Shelli—liked her enough to hire her for her own company. The strong bond of people re-hiring the same person, working together over long periods of time, is significant. It shows that those people care enough about you to keep you around, that they want you to be a part of whatever it is that they are doing.

Further, Shelli's resume shows a clear predisposition toward working with people. Her work as a Residential Advisor in college, and as a camp counselor, shows that she has an effective and meaningful way of dealing with people. That she was promoted to Resident Advisor Coordinator shows that she is capable of managing people efficiently. While this may seem irrelevant at first, understand that ALL experience, no matter how diverse, has relevance and application to this industry.

Shelli is also smart to indicate her language, art history and computer skills. Often, these skills are called into play, no matter how obscure they seem. Further, these skills serve to illustrate who she is as a person. Shelli is not just a two-dimensional PA candidate when she lets us know that she speaks Italian and can tell the difference between a Goya and a C-stand.

Tania Alvarez

56809 Pico Blvd. # 303
Los Angeles, CA 90036
Tel: 323/555-9288

EXPERIENCE:

2004 *Wardrobe Intern*
Always Remember (Feature Film) F1Productions
Costume Designer: Maryann Doheny; Director: Rex Clavins
Period: 1960s, rural South—Civil rights movement

2004 *Wardrobe Assistant*
Boyz on the Run (Short Film) Shoes Up Productions
Costume Designer: Lydia Donza; Director: Chase Besinger
Period: Contemporary, urban hip-hop

2003 *Costumer*
Cruise This! (AFI Student Film) Big Show Productions
Costume Designer: Holly Dria; Director: Elisa Boffle
Period: Contemporary, professional sailing community

2003 *Costume Designer*
Cha-Cha Blues (Student Film) CCAC Productions
Period: Contemporary with flashbacks to 1970s, dance movie with 50 extras and 5 principals. *Audience Award, 2001 Danzfylm Festival, Bonn, Germany.*

EDUCATION:

California College of Arts and Crafts, San Francisco, CA
Bachelor of Arts in Textile Design 2003

OTHER:

Expert Patterning and Tailoring skills
Extensive knowledge of period tailoring and accessories
Internet-savvy and proficient with Costume Pro (MAC)

References available on request

Tania is applying for a costumer position on a low-budget, non-union film. Her resume is going to look and feel different from the two we have just seen. Tania has recently graduated from an arts college, and wants to represent her diverse experience with the craft of costuming. She tells us, with this resume, that she has worn a number of hats in her field. She has been the responsible one, the costume designer, and she has worked for other people in the capacity of costumer, assistant and intern. From this list, it appears that Tania would have the experience to be a self-sufficient team player. It's good that Tania listed her design credit; it tells the interviewer that she can handle the mantle of responsibility and that she can be accountable for her work.

Further, her major in textile design is an interesting spin to bring to the costume table. It will certainly provide Tania with insight into fabric choices when the costume designer starts shopping for swatches. Tania would be the obvious choice for a fabric consultant, given her background, and with her expert patterning and tailoring skills, she's a shoo-in on a show where construction of costumes is required. Further, Tania's listing of a relevant computer program skill, Costume Pro, and her familiarity with the internet, are going to be huge plusses. Believe it or not, there are people in the entertainment industry who do not own computers. Your computer skills, if you have them, will go a long way in making you more efficient and more marketable. Don't sell yourself short. If you have skills, list them!

SLAM-DUNKING THE INTERVIEW

Here's the deal: know your shit and shine, shine, shine. Study all you can about the company, its employees, their clientele and the way they do business. Research them in the trades, on imdb.com, and on the rest of the internet. Read books that deal with their history or their projects. If you are interviewing with a filmmaker, study their body of work, memorize their past accomplishments. Go out and rent the films they worked on. Educate yourself about their methods.

If you are interviewing for a position that requires you to show examples of your work, whether it be a portfolio or a "reel" (a DVD or video tape with your work edited to music), make it sing!! Presentation is everything; this is a primarily visual medium, and interviewers love to be dazzled. Make sure that your portfolio pages are well-designed and laid out clearly to display your work in the best manner. If you have a reel, you will want a catchy song and flashy editing, with your contact information displayed prominently at the end.

Interviewers will ask some strange questions sometimes, including things like: "What do you consider your greatest weakness?" or "What do you absolutely hate to do?" Rather than answer with a blank stare, you might want to think of some clever answers to the so-called trick questions in advance. If you can think of a funny answer, all the better. Some people have been known to put interviewees on the spot to see how they react, and if you came back with humor, you win.

Interviewers will often ask what your favorite films, directors and actors are—they want to know the breadth of your knowledge of the industry, and they want to get a handle on your taste in projects. It helps to be well-read, but having a vast knowledge of the product (whether it be film or television) is extremely helpful. You will be able to speak a common language during the interview, referencing stories, visual images or dialogue that will inform the interviewer that you know your shit.

THE RULES

When you do arrive at some kind of job placement, whether it is an internship or an entry-level job, there is a set of rules you need to know about. Follow them, and your early career will be drama-free and well-managed. Ignore them, and take your chances.

1) <u>Always be early</u>

   No matter what, always-always-always arrive early to work. It is great to be on time, but being early is even better. Being early to work demonstrates that you are excited to be doing what you are doing. Your boss will notice, believe me. Being early will also afford you a few moments to mentally prepare for the day, get a cup of coffee, and get up to speed. You will perform better overall if you have had the chance to wake up a bit before the work day starts. If, for any reason, you believe that you may be even five minutes late, call your supervisor IMMEDIATELY and explain the situation. The entertainment industry runs like clockwork, and every minute counts, particularly in production. If you are consistently late to work on a show or commercial, you will be terminated. There is a zero-tolerance policy for tardiness in production.

2) <u>Have a Positive Mental Attitude</u>

   You spend sixteen hours a day with your coworkers. No matter how talented you are or how refined your skills, a bad attitude will

ALWAYS be a detriment to the work environment. There are many, many people in this industry who would rather hire "fun" people than skilled people. Remember this. Your talent and skill will get you nowhere if you are a drag to be around. If you find yourself tired, dirty and beat after a long day, remember that your attitude is your CHOICE. No one forces you to be a jerk. You choose your behavior. Your employers may forget a small mistake committed last week, but they will remember a bad attitude for years. Word-of-mouth can spread as well, so choose your attitude wisely. A positive, fun employee will consistently find work; a negative, drag of an employee will not. Keep your whining and complaining to yourself.

3) Be Proactive in Problem-Solving and Finding Creative Solutions
There are going to be a hundred problems a day that come up on the job, no matter what branch of the industry you choose. Finding solutions to the problems, creating new and efficient ways to handle the recurring ones, will go very far in strengthening your work relationships. Making entertainment is a team effort, and the more you can do to demonstrate "team spirit"—making things easier not just for yourself or your immediate counterparts, but for EVERYONE—the farther you will go. Individual achievement is truly impossible in entertainment; every achievement is the result of a group effort. Do what you can to make it better for everyone, and everyone (including yourself) wins.

4) Be Honest and Trustworthy
Your employers are going to entrust you with many things: private home phone numbers and addresses of their celebrity clients, personal details of their lives, house keys, car keys, petty cash, secret projects or scripts, it goes on and on. The quickest way to lose a job is to betray your employer's trust. Trust is earned, and people in this business are not going to be quick to give it to you. You will need to prove yourself to your employer and your co-workers. When someone tells you a secret or entrusts you with confidential information, KEEP IT TO YOURSELF. When someone entrusts you with their car keys, house keys, large amounts of petty cash, be responsible. Do not steal property or ideas. Do not sell photographs or information to The Enquirer, the Star or the Globe. Do not copy or distribute dailies and/or rough cuts of films. Do not post forbidden pictures from the set on Ain't it Cool. A breach of trust is grounds for losing your job immediately.

5) Be Dependable and Consistent

You may lack the natural talent or superior training to perform your job tasks masterfully, but if you can demonstrate consistent efforts to improve and contribute on the job, you will be rewarded. Show up early; ask what needs to be done; admit when you don't know the answers; seek the answers to what you don't know; inform your boss when you're going to lunch, how long you will be, and how to reach you; complete every task given to you *thoroughly*; ask for feedback; keep your desk or work area organized; keep your paperwork organized; admit when you are overwhelmed and need help; communicate regularly in person, on the phone, and via email—not just to your co-workers and clients, but to your boss; keep your lunch time to an hour or less (lunch is usually anywhere from 1 PM to 3 PM); keep personal phone calls at work to a bare minimum; provide cheerful help to your co-workers without someone having to ask you to do it; make sure your boss knows when you are leaving at the end of each day, and how to reach you in an emergency. You don't have to be a Fulbright scholar to be successful on the job; apply yourself consistently and you will succeed.

6) Demonstrate Gratitude and Respect

This is a competitive business. For every one job opening at Agency X, there are a thousand people who would kill to have it. When someone does something kind for you, recommends you for a job or does something helpful, acknowledge it. You don't have to be obsequious in your gratitude, but help is priceless, and one nice turn deserves a thank-you card at minimum. The thank-you card means more to people than you realize. You may want to invest in some nice, beautiful and/or unusual stationery for these thank-you notes. If the card is really outstanding, the recipient might save it or display it in his/her office, and remember you for it. If that recipient is the head of a studio, that recognition could mean a lot to you (professionally) in years to come. No one is obligated to do you any favors, and it is a sign of your respect (for that person) to acknowledge their kindness. Anyone who is in a position to do you a work-related favor deserves respect, for they have succeeded in some fashion and are giving back. If you can remember to be kind, respectful and fair in your own dealings, you will be well-served. Try to avoid stepping on other people's toes, and making them mad. The oft-repeated proverb here is "The toes you tread on today may be attached to the ass you have to kiss tomorrow", but the entertainment industry is a small world; what comes around, goes around. Kissing ass, or groveling, is not a part of any job description, but demonstrating respect and courtesy is crucial.

7) <u>Actively Discourage Gossip</u>
Gossip is the great invisible cancer in the workplace. Things that are said can never be unsaid, and things that are heard (or overheard) can never be purged from memory. Lasting impressions and opinions are easily formed about people and situations based on gossip, which may or may not have roots in the truth. Gossip is destructive and poisonous to a team. It undermines the sense of unity, family, and trust created in a working team environment. The proliferation of rumors and the passing along of gossip should be avoided and prevented at all costs. If you hear gossip in the work environment, change the subject. There are a hundred other things to talk about than someone else's business. Keep your side of the street clean, and you will be respected for it. If you work with an individual who is an incessant gossip, you may choose to have a word with him/her. It is perfectly reasonable to inform the person of your distaste for gossip, and to politely but firmly ask the offender to stop.

8) <u>Never, EVER, Date a Co-Worker While You Are Still Working Together</u>
You are guaranteed to break this rule at least once in your career. We have all done it, and we have ALL learned the very painful lesson of rule number eight: wait until the show is *over* before you date a co-worker. If you work in an office, wait until one of you transfers to a different location or different company. You can go so far as to express interest, get to know each other well, talk about your respective painful childhoods, but *hands off the merchandise* until they call wrap! Why? Sixteen hour days, day after day, week after week, month after month, together. Problems and/or issues are bound to arise in your relationship that, in the heat of sleep deprivation and production, can become volatile and make you miserable. But you still have to go to work, and there is no escape from your co-worker, or the miserable situation. There are, more often than not, location romances on film sets. This situation is often worse, and more intense, because the crew is together 24 hours a day, seven days a week, sequestered in the same hotel. Tread carefully and be patient. If a relationship is meant to work, it will withstand the waiting period for your job to be finished.

9) Get A Decent Amount Of Sleep
This may be the key to all of the rules. Sleep deprivation is a real danger to your health, your safety, and to your productivity. In general, people are more irritable and less able to focus and perform when they have consistently been deprived of adequate sleep. Excessive hours in production may cause your sleep patterns to become erratic, but in the interest of your well-being, you need to ensure that you get enough sleep to avoid catastrophe. There have been instances of exhausted crew members being killed in accidents while driving home from work, asleep at the wheel. If you are exhausted at this level, you will need to supplement your sleep. Some people nap on their lunch hour. In severe cases, some crews sleep or take naps in shifts to provide enough rest during production. Even if you think you can handle it, closing down bars or staying out late every night after work will impact your sleep (and your productivity) dramatically. Your bosses will know if you are tired, hung over and sleep-deprived. Coming in to work in this condition is a huge no-no, and grounds for termination. Take care of yourself.

10) Always Do Your Best Work; You Never Know Who's Watching.
Literally, you never know who's watching, whether it's on-screen or at the office. Building a good reputation is your responsibility, but also partially based on how you are perceived by the people who see you in action. If you keep in mind that everything you do, *everything*, reflects upon your character and your abilities, and that everyone you encounter could potentially impact your life, either positively or negatively, based on your behavior, you are understanding the concept. The casual stranger who asks you how you like your boss may be the new CEO of the company, unbeknownst to you at the time. The catering chef on the small film you're working on may be producing movies next year, and want to hire you. You never know who is monitoring your career progress, waiting for you to be available. Be on your toes, doing your best work, and capitalize on the opportunities that come your way as a result.

CELEBRITIES

A word on dealing with celebrities in the work environment: don't be a dork. Celebrities—whether they are actors, directors, producers, writers, rock stars or reality TV participants—are just people. They have the same insecurities, fears, desires, doubts, and concerns as you do. The difference is that they are famous and you are not. To put such a person on a pedestal, or worse, to allow yourself to be "star-struck" in their presence, would be an egregious mistake. Celebrities are a huge and necessary part of the work environment in the entertainment industry. They are also part of the fabric of everyday life in Hollywood. You may be standing in line behind George Clooney at Starbucks one morning, and reclining in a dentist chair next to Christina Applegate the next. You will become accustomed to these experiences. When you are working with celebrities, treat them with the same respect you would treat anyone else in their position. Do not ask them for their autograph, unless you are really comfortable asking the person, and know that it would not be an inconvenience. There are many gracious celebrities who would love to sign autographs all day at work, but you never know who is *into* it and who is *annoyed* by it. Be respectful, and give celebrities professional and personal space.

GROW A RHINO HIDE

In your quest for a successful industry career, you need to know one thing: not everyone is going to be nice to you. In fact, a lot of people in this business are downright ornery, mean-spirited, and condescending. Your assignment, from day one, will be to cultivate a skin so thick, not even the acrylic nails of ego, greed, and jealousy can pierce it. One helpful hint to thicken your skin is to consider the source of disparaging remarks, and to not take them too seriously. Most people who are fool enough to be giant knuckleheads ought not to be considered credible sources of criticism. Some people have anger problems, and will use you as their outlet for depraved rage and demonic outbursts. The bitter drink of personal dissatisfaction has poisoned others, and they spit venom. Consider the profound impact of these peoples' sadness and disappointment on their behavior, and let their remarks roll right off your leathery hide. Furthermore, make a sincere effort not to hold grudges. It is a waste of energy. Eventually, you may learn to not get too emotional about work, and that would be a good thing.

THE WORKING LIFE

What should you expect on the job? Expect long hours, no matter what field you choose. Expect a 9—7 day for a desk job, and sometimes working nights and weekends in the crunch time. Expect a certain amount of bullshit from the people with whom you work and with the people they are trying to impress. Expect good days and bad days. Beyond that, cast aside your expectations. Be realistic and open to new perspectives on what you are doing. Your experience will not be like anyone else's, ever before. You will have your own Hollywood stories to tell in time.

Once you have found a job that suits you, the next step is to make yourself invaluable, but not to the point where you are irreplaceable. Should you be perceived as irreplaceable in your position, you may not move up as quickly as you like. People in Hollywood are quick to pigeon-hole, and it may not serve you well. The best bet for quick, upward mobility is to be diligent, driven, to innovate, and work hard. If you have talent, do good work and persevere, even in the most competitive climate, you will eventually be rewarded. If you can blossom in your new job, if you enjoy it, and if there is room for you to grow, hold on to it. Good jobs are a blessing.

When you have found a career path that suits you, it is time to make some goals. Sit down with a notepad and pen and decide what you would like to achieve in the next five years. Be specific and to-the-point; the list doesn't have to be lengthy or highly detailed. Commit to doing your best to making those goals happen, and refer to the list every few months if you need to. If you know what you want to do, it is easier to achieve.

WHEN TO WALK AWAY

You may find yourself, at some point, in a job that makes you miserable. When should you walk away? There are a few situations that would warrant serious consideration for leaving your job, and they include: sexual harassment, physical threats, verbal abuse, pervasive drug use (by your boss or close associates), unsafe/dangerous work conditions, mental illness or burnout due to extreme levels of stress. If you witness or are a victim of any of the above behavior that is technically illegal, you should first inform the head of Human Resources (at the company) or the Producer (on a production) before deciding whether or not to go to the police. It would be very, very rare that legal action be leveled against an employer or coworker in the entertainment industry for abuse as mentioned above. No one really wants the negative publicity or legal expense. Don't let that stop you from filing a report, however, if the abuse is serious and criminal by definition.

Alternately, do not conduct yourself in a criminal manner on the job—be very careful about protecting your boss and your co-workers' privacy. Stories fly around Hollywood about personal assistants' egregious errors in judgment with respect to their employers. Examples include selling the celebrity employer's used clothing on eBay (without celebrity knowing), manufacturing t-shirts with celebrity's likeness and "quotes of the day" (without celebrity knowing or authorizing), giving celebrity home tours when celebrity is out of town, reserving tables at restaurants using celebrity's name and credit card, and so forth. You will be *so* fired, *so* fast.

You may also consider leaving a position when you feel that the opportunity for career advancement has passed, or when you feel that people are consistently taking advantage of you. To avoid getting stuck in a "plateau" position, or one in which you are constantly burdened with other peoples' work, you might decide to shake things up a little bit and pursue other opportunities within your field. This type of change can prove very beneficial, forcing you to put your own wind in your sails.

Knowing when to leave a job, even one that has been good to you, is difficult. Consider the financial ramifications carefully. Save enough money to tide you over for a few months (at least) until you find a new job. The easiest thing to do would be to find another job *before* you leave your current position, but make sure that you do not exit suddenly, leaving your current employer in the lurch. It is very important NOT to burn bridges; Los Angeles is a very small place. Word travels fast and forever if you screw someone over.

CONCLUSION

The most important thing is to dig in to your new job, your new career, and make the most of your opportunities. Study the rules of conduct, and follow them! Make goals and do your best to realize them. Remember to be diplomatic and gracious. Do your homework, know your shit, and kick ass. The rest will take care of itself.

INTERVIEW

Subject: Jordan Levine
CEO, Celluloid Heroes

Hometown: Brooklyn, NY
Moved to LA: 1989

Topic: Finding your Niche

Where did you go & what did you study in college?

I went to Pratt Institute in Brooklyn, NY, and studied Film for a BFA.

How did you decide to come to LA?

After graduation I moved back home; two days later a friend of mine called and said he was going to LA, and asked if I would like to join him. I did not hesitate.

Describe your first living situation:

My friend got hooked up with CSUN *(California State University at Northridge)* to live in the dorms at Northridge. We were supposed to pay for the summer in advance, but when we showed up there was no one available to take our check (it was July 4th weekend and I guess everyone took a long weekend). We got an RA to let us in. The place smelled very bad. There was some sort of leak and the carpets were wet and smelled very musky. We realized very fast that Northridge on the map looked a lot closer to the heart of Hollywood than it was it real life. We knew we had to get out. We went driving around the new hood, ended up on the 101 and saw Coldwater Canyon. It sounded like a cool street name so we just got off. 1.5 minutes off the freeway we saw a "for rent" sign. The place was perfect: two bedrooms, one bath and $700 per month. We had no furniture, TV, dishes; really we had nothing. The place looked just the apartment in *The Karate Kid.*

What was your first job in LA & how did you get it?

My first job was as a runner at 21st Century Films. My father has a friend whose son worked in Hollywood. He was a trailer editor at Cimarron *(a large trailer editing house)* at the time. I called him out of the blue. He was nice enough and told me that he could get me a job at Cimarron as a runner, but the people in charge of the runners were terrible and the company was hard to move up in. So he, in turn, gave me a phone number of one his friends, who in turn gave me another number, who in turn gave another number and then I ended up interviewing for the runner job at 21st Century Films. At first I don't think the woman I interviewed with wanted to hire me. (She said) "You don't know L.A.—you are new to town!"

I said—with great confidence—that that is what maps are for. I called her the next morning to check in, with the attitude that I already had the job, I mean, why wouldn't someone hire me?! Not to sound cocky; I think I was just naive about how the world worked. (Later on I was just cocky). She gave the ole "ummm this and that," but somehow she ended saying, "Well, O.K., see you tomorrow."

I loved being a runner. I got to learn LA—and real fast. I knew all the sound and video houses. Met people that I am still good friends with and had a blast.

Did you have any inkling you wanted to be an editor?

When I lived in NY I was working as a production electric. I had fun, but always wanted to edit. I always loved editing in college. When I came out, it was a new start. I could have done anything. Lucky for me I became a runner in the post-production department of 21st Century. So, once the first job happened, it was like a domino effect for the rest of my career.

What was your first editing job in LA?

21st Century was creating an in-house marketing department. The guy in charge, Chris Dobbs, already had an assistant hired, but at the last moment he (the assistant) took another gig and left Chris hangin'. I think I was the nearest warm body. Chris was also the only one in all of Hollywood that cared that I went to "film school". Before I knew it, I was working with him. The great thing about 21st for me was that they were small and that they were "cheap fuckers". That meant that they couldn't afford a *real* assistant and were left with me. I got a chance to do everything: go to mixes, on line, telecines, deal with editors, producers.... I only worked there eight months, but got years of experience.

Side note: I realized after a year of working in the real world that life was over as I knew it. So I quit my job, got in my car and drove across the country for three months. Ran up the credit cards, but had the time of my life. I had three months of just roaming the county. It was a great time.

When did you make the decision to solely edit trailers (as opposed to features)?

I just fell into trailers. But I did love it. Good for my personality. I worked at Corman (*Concorde-New Horizons, Roger Corman's company)* on one feature. Had fun, met the girl of my dreams, and then met Holly :) (*Note: Holly is Jordan's wife*). Work wise, I did not like the idea of working of features. Mainly since most movies suck. I couldn't dream of being stuck on one film for months and have to pretend that it was good. In trailers, we do nothing but bag on the shit movies that we work on. I love taking the crap and making a kick-ass trailer. Although, it's always better to work on a good movie and make a kick-ass trailer.

How long did you work at someone else's trailer company?

After Corman/Concorde, I was bouncing around as a freelance finisher. Then quit again and hung out with a bunch of friends that came to LA to visit for a few weeks. In June 1991, I ended up at Cimarron. I was an assistant there for about a year and a half and then become an editor. I cut there for six years, working on many major theatrical releases. (That was when I was in my cocky stage) I always had the attitude that I was doing them a favor by working there. I find this attitude, to a degree, keeps a healthy mental balance toward work. I never, like so many that I know, let the job define me or control me.

When did you get the notion that you could start your own trailer company?

I always liked being in the thick of it. I loved trailers and wanted more control of how they were created: dealing with clients, that sort of thing. But it was really more stupidity than anything else. I never really thought too much about how to do…it just happened. I told Holly, my wife, that maybe in five years I would like to start something. We went to a party, and I bumped into Glenn Garland (*another editor*) who told me about the Shah Brothers *(Ash and Sundip Shah, movie producers/distributors)*. He (Glenn) was unavailable to cut a trailer for them and told them about me. I called, cut one trailer for them; they were blown away. I think it was the first time that they had a trailer cut by a real trailer person. I then told Holly that I started the company and that was that.

How did you get the money and backing to start your own business?

As an editor at one of the largest trailer houses in Hollywood, I made great money. I also had low monthly expenses. So for months I socked away the cash. While doing this, I was still working at Cimarron during the day. At night I worked for Celluloid Heroes. I also took out a home line of credit against the house so that we could afford our first Avid. Then I finally left Cimarron and got my first Avid system.

Where did you find your first clients, and how do you find them now?

The first client was the Shahs. I got very very very very lucky. They loved working with me. Right as I started, they started a home video distribution business. I was cutting 25 trailers a year. They really built Celluloid Heroes. They put me in touch with Paramount Pay Television. Holly, my wife, used to be a producer, and while reading the trades one day noticed something about (writer/director) Bill Condon and *Gods and Monsters*. She knew one of his assistants. We got him a reel. Bill hated the trailer that Lions Gate was doing for his film. We told him we would do one on spec. He loved it; Lions Gate loved it. So within 16 months we had one huge volume client, one kind-of studio client (Paramount Pay Television), and one art house client. It stayed that way for years.

Fast forward years later…I do everything from cold calling, asking clients to tell their friends about us, and talking to everyone that will listen. Many people also just call us. Sometimes it amazes me that people have actually heard of us. Also, clients leave one company and go to another. If we are lucky, we will still work with the original company and start working with the client in their new company. A big lesson I learned years ago: you cannot neglect your current clients. Don't assume that they will always work with you. There is always someone else banging on their door to get their business.

How has it been going for you?

Not too bad.

CHAPTER FOUR

FRIENDS

Friends can make the difference between a happy experience of Los Angeles and a dreadful one. Friends become your surrogate family when you are far from home, building a new life. For all the grumbling you may hear about people in Los Angeles being "fake", I would like to dispel the myth. There are plenty of wonderful, genuine people here in Los Angeles. The trouble, sometimes, is finding them. When you make good friends, keep them close. Choose your friends carefully and dump the fakes.

You may arrive in Los Angeles with friends from college or your hometown. You may set up life together in an apartment, preparing to be best buddies for life. The honest truth is that things may not work out the way you plan. People change and grow. Working in the entertainment industry is stressful and time-consuming. The business can change your priorities and what you want from life. Sometimes, we run out of time to maintain every last one of our old friendships. From my own experience, I can tell you that I am no longer in contact with the college buddies who moved to LA when I did. I don't hold it against them, and I wouldn't suspect they would hold it against me. Our lives simply went in different directions. As you work and encounter new types of people, you will make new friends who share your passions.

SEEKING FRIENDS

In making new friends, seek *good* friends, not political ones. Political friends, or friends whose sole purpose in your life is to afford influence in your career, are fake friends. Good friends are good friends. Business associates are business associates. This is part of the problem with the perception that people in LA are "fake". Many people fail to make the distinction between "friend" and "business associate" because they want to be perceived as "similar to" this fake friend. Good friends, friends with whom you share common goals, interests, values and passions, will benefit you far more than political friends in the end because they will enrich your *life*, not just your career. Many people miss this point, but it is a crucial one. Your good friends comprise your emotional experience and your family environment; your friends are really your world here.

WORKPLACE FRIENDSHIPS

You never know where some of your best friends will be lurking. You may meet them at work. Many a lifelong friendship has been forged in the early stages of an entertainment career. Working side-by-side with your buddy in the mailroom at Agency X today, running a studio together tomorrow. The work environment can allow mutual respect and intellectual understanding to flourish. Choose these work-friends carefully.

It is perfectly acceptable, and often encouraged, to go out for dinner, drinks, parties with your co-workers. However, you should be aware of your limits. Occasionally, too much alcohol or recreational intoxicants can cause embarrassing and erratic behavior that, in the light of day, makes the workplace awkward for a time. Be careful in the early stages of your work friendships not to get so wasted that you make an ass out of yourself and say something out of turn to your co-workers.

With regard to becoming close friends with your co-workers, exercise prudence. On-the-job familiarity sometimes breeds contempt, and what once was a delightful friendship turns into an irritating obligation. Sometimes, in getting to know someone, you see their true colors and it is too much information. This is a precarious situation at work. While it is good to develop genuine friendships at work, there is a hazard to having your co-workers know so much about you that, if they wanted to, they could one day turn that information into ammunition. I have seen it happen, and it is not pretty. Choose your work friends carefully.

NETWORKING

Your social circle will undoubtedly contain elements of your work life. Friends introduce you to their friends, and your professional and social networking connections will grow. There are many people here in Hollywood who would have you believe that the key to success is networking, but they are only partially correct. In order to really be successful, you must learn to network well, without being false or manipulative.

A strong web of social connections can open doors for you professionally. When you meet new professional connections in a social environment, remember that you are meeting SOCIALLY. Many people do not like to "talk shop" at happy hour. If you can connect with someone socially, and then, in developing your relationship over time, parlay it into a professional relationship, you have succeeded in networking. It may take months or years for a social connection to develop into a professional relationship, but when it happens, you will have had the opportunity to get to know your new contact well enough to work better together.

People in Hollywood can see right through a bad networker. If you have an agenda that you are trying to push, you will be sniffed out immediately. This usually breeds resentment in the target of your networking. S/he may remember this infraction and be annoyed by it for a long time, and will likely never return your phone calls. If you have made a networking mistake, apologize succinctly and leave the person alone. If you apologize too much, you may appear desperate. Be professional; cut your losses and move on.

NON-INDUSTRY FRIENDS

You may find new friends through extra-curricular activities, or through friends of your friends. It is always a good idea to have friends outside of your field of work. Life is pretty dull when there is no fresh perspective. These non-industry friends can be a tremendous asset to your sense of being grounded and centered.

GROWING, CHANGING FRIENDSHIPS

The close friends you choose in your early twenties may not be the close friends you hold dear in your thirties. People change; their priorities shift. Your friends will take new jobs, get successful, move to a new neighborhood, fall in love, get married, start families—and not necessarily in that order. These life changes will seriously impact who they become as people. Suddenly your frat-boy party friend wants to spend his weekends with his new girlfriend, who becomes his fiancée, who becomes his wife and the mother of his children. And somewhere in there, he went from working as a PA to working as a camera assistant, to working for Panavision, to living in Monrovia, and you never see him any more. This is part of life, part of growing with and without your friendships. Try not to take it personally. If it's a friendship worth holding on to, do what you can to keep the lines of communication open; there may come a time when you can reconnect fully. It is important to have the grace to let your friends become the people they want to be, and the people they are destined to become.

BEING A GOOD FRIEND

It may seem obvious, how to be a good friend…but is it, really? Here in Los Angeles, where all the dream-chasers converge, how do you maintain friendships? With all of us wrapped up in our own pursuits, how can we possibly give of ourselves and maintain our support systems? In being a good friend, we give each other steadiness, fidelity, love and support—the things we are supposed to get from our families.

Do nice things for others, not just for your friends. It will make you feel good, and it will make the other person feel supported and cared-for. The happiness derived from doing a good deed is contagious. Do spontaneous good deeds for your friends, without being asked. Offer to help them with their taxes, water their plants when they're away, treat them to lunch, remember them on their birthday, listen to them when they need an ear. Make time to be together often. Take care of each other; you're family.

If your friends are putting up plays, screening their films, or playing gigs, go to see them. Support your friends in their professional, as well as personal endeavors. Show up. When you say you are going to do something, do it. Do not be a flake: follow through and be dependable. If you make promises to your friends, keep them.

Tell the truth diplomatically. Never, ever lie to your friends. There are too many duplicitous people in the entertainment industry already. Let your friends know where they can get their truth served straight up. Confront your friends when they mess up. Help them up when they stumble. Regard your friendships as sacred. Respect your friends' desires for space and private time, and forgive them if they stress out once in a while. Be a good friend, and you will have good friends.

One important aspect to retaining good friendships is creating "family time" together. Spend time with your friends cooking dinner, watching movies, walking, going to museums, or just getting together to watch TV. Try not to get sucked into the vortex of work. Make familial human contact a daily feature in your life. Remember and celebrate religious events that are important to you. Visit with the families of your friends—including the older folks and children—and really get to know them. Forge the bonds of love and support that will make your life a happy one, no matter what curves life, and the entertainment industry, throw your way.

INTERVIEW

Subject: Jon Favreau
Actor, Writer, Director, Producer
Credits include: ***Swingers, Made, Elf***

Hometown: Queens, NY
Moved to LA: 1992

Topic: Role of Friendship

Describe your decision to move to LA—did you know anyone here?

We had just finished shooting *Rudy* and I came out for pilot season. I told the producers of *Rudy* that I was coming to town, and they set me up with meetings with agents. I had met Vince (Vaughn) on the set of *Rudy* and he lived here, so we hung out a lot. The producers of *Rudy* introduced me to the business side of things and Vince showed me the town.

Describe your first living situation:

I shared a house on Melrose with an actress that I had met at an improv show through mutual friends. I paid half the rent and she had nine tenths of the house. I slept on a futon on the floor. The only thing I had in the room was my computer. All I did was play Tetris.

Describe your first job in LA:

I was already established as an actor so I didn't need to work per se. I did storyboards for Sean Astin on his short film, *Kangaroo Court*, which was nominated for an Oscar. Sean and his wife ran their production offices. I was impressed by how they could run a company with so little money. It probably served as an inspiration on some level with *Swingers*, which I did, years later, on the same level.

What friends did you have in town when you moved here, and how did you meet new friends?

I already knew Vince and through him I met Peter Billingsley. Ron Livingston had moved out a month before I had and I had met him through dressing up as Captain Crunch at a boat show in Chicago. He was living on a chicken ranch in Reseda with some friends of the family from back in Iowa.

What role did these friends play in your writing?

I based the characters in *Swingers* on many of them. Thinking of how they would talk gave me an ear for the dialogue, and the experiences we had inspired events in the movie.

Also, Ron Livingston was the first person I showed the script to. His reaction to my writing gave me the confidence to send the script to my agent.

What role did your friends play in getting *Swingers* off the ground?

The friends of mine who I based characters on all pulled together to do staged readings to help procure financing. Although none of the readings led to any breaks or cash per se, they helped me develop a vision for the film and made it easier to shoot when we finally did get the financing. The readings served as a rehearsal period for the year and half prior to the cameras rolling.

Describe what it is like to do business with your friends—is it easier (because you have an existent friendly relationship) or more difficult (because people are sensitive, business-is-business)?

I think it is more difficult, at least speaking for myself. Rarely, if ever, will I approach a friend for a favor. If I am going to ask someone who is a friend for something on a professional level, I make sure it is a mutually beneficial situation. I want to make sure it works for everyone.

Did your relationships with your friends change after or during the time when your work was getting a lot of attention?

In the case of *Swingers* it was exponentially bizarre. It was hitting for all of us at the same time. Not only did I have to deal with my entire frame of reference changing, my friends were facing the same turmoil. I remember one day I was driving on Sunset Blvd. and Vince was driving in the opposite direction. Vince had been getting a lot of work off *Swingers* and I was getting many offers to write and direct. We should have been happy. I yelled to him and asked him how he was doing, he yelled to me, "Miserable." I yelled back, "Me too." We weren't kidding.

How has your relationship with your friends changed since you married and have had children?

When you have kids, everything else is a distant second.

Any surprises/anything else?

As a rule, I find that most people aren't as smart as you think they are going to be.

CHAPTER FIVE

HOBBIES and EXTRACURRICULARS

Believe it or not, there is more to life than work. I know, it sounds so inconceivable when you have such passion for your career! It is vital to your mental, emotional and physical well-being to find pursuits outside of the entertainment industry. In exploring your options, you may have opportunities to meet new people, make new friends and business connections, and have a fuller, richer life.

Los Angeles offers a wealth of activities, what I like to call *extracurricular activities*, that include everything from the Lakers to the Opera, children's charity to spiritual clarity. Whatever you want to do to wind down or get away, you will find it here in Los Angeles.

RECREATIONAL ATHLETICS

Whether you join a gym or study yoga, you will be thrilled to have a release for some of your physical stress. Los Angeles' beautiful weather provides ample opportunity for outdoor recreation nearly year-round. The following are some local opportunities for the athlete in you:

GYMS—Los Angeles has several major chains, some listed below:

- 24 Hour Fitness 800/204-2400
- Bally's 800/846-0256
- Bodies in Motion 310/264-0777
- Crunch 323/654-4550
- Gold's Gym (Hollywood) 323/462-7012
- Gold's Gym (Venice) 310/392-6004
- Sports Club LA 310/473-1447

- YMCA Hollywood 323/467-4161
- YMCA West LA 310/477-1511

SWIMMING—Public pools for adult lap swim (some have Master's programs):

- Cleveland (Reseda) 818/756-9798
- Echo Indoor (Downtown) 213/481-2640
- Hubert Humphrey (Pacoima) 818/896-0067
- Roosevelt (4th & Soto, East LA) 213/485-7391
- Venice Rec. Center Pool 310/575-8260
- Westwood Rec. Center Pool 310/478-7019
- YMCA Hollywood 323/467-4161
- YMCA West Los Angeles 310/477-1511

YOGA STUDIOS—They vary in price, dependent on area:

- Bikram's Yoga College of India 310/854-5800
- Golden Bridge 323/936-4172
- Maha Yoga, Brentwood 310/899-0047
- Marc Blanchard Power Yoga 310/441-3773
- Valley Yoga, Studio City 818/788-9642
- Yoga Works, Santa Monica 310/393-5150

TENNIS—the city is peppered with free, and pay, courts:

FREE COURTS (on a first-come, first-served basis)

- 12621 Rye St., Studio City, CA 91604
- 1341 Lake St., Venice 90291
- 1632 Bellevue Ave., Echo Park 90026
- 16953 Ventura Blvd. Encino 91316
- 1835 Stoner Ave, West Los Angeles, 90025
- 333 S. Barrington, Brentwood 90049
- 4702 N. Figueroa St., Los Angeles 90042
- 5301 Tujunga Ave., North Hollywood 91601

PAY COURTS (reservations accepted with City of LA tennis card)

- Balboa: 17015 Burbank Blvd., Encino 91316 818/995-6570
- Beverly Hills: 325 S. La Cienega 310/652-7555
- Cheviot Hills: 2551 Motor Ave., LA 90064 310/836-8879
- Silverlake: 2715 Vermont Canyon, LA 90027 323/664-3521
- Van Nuys: 14201 Huston St., Van Nuys 91423 818/756-8400
- Westwood: 1350 Sepulveda, LA 90024 310/575-8299

GOLF—The following are public courses. Greens fees vary, but most are very affordable, and cheaper on weekdays than weekends.

- Encino/Balboa (2 18-hole courses) 818/995-1170
- Holmby Park (pitch-n-putt) 310/276-1604
- Penmar (9 holes) 310/396-6228
- Rancho Park (18 holes) 310/838-7373
- Rancho Park (9 holes) 310/838-7561
- Roosevelt (9 holes) 323/665-2011
- Van Nuys (18 hole short course) 818/785-8871
- Whitsett (pitch-n-putt) 818/761-3250
- Wilson & Harding (2 18-hole courses) 323/663-2555

BATTING CAGES—Available on a pay-per hour basis

- Burbank: Batcade 818/842-6455
- Culver City: Slamo Baseball 310/398-5050
- Glendale: Glendale Batting Cages 818/243-2363
- Sherman Oaks: Castle Batting Park 818/905-1321
- Van Nuys: Bat-A-Way 818/786-1600

BASKETBALL—Adult league play is available through the following:

- G/M Sports Office/City of Los Angeles
  Men's and Women's leagues, all levels, two seasons per year.
  818/246-5613

ICE HOCKEY—Adult league play is available through the following:

- Iceoplex Hockey League (all levels)
  Panorama Ice, Van Nuys
  818/893-1784
- Culver City Hockey League
  Culver City Ice Rink, Culver City
  310/398-5718

BASEBALL—Adult league play is available through the following:

- Valley Sports Office/City of Los Angeles
  Men's and Women's leagues, all levels, two seasons per year.
  818/765-0284

SOFTBALL—Adult league play is available through the following:

- Valley Sports Office/City of Los Angeles
  and Women's leagues, all levels, two seasons per year.
  818/765-0284

VOLLEYBALL—Adult league play is available through the following:

- G/M Sports Office/City of Los Angeles
  Men's and Women's leagues, all levels, two seasons per year.
  818/246-5613

SOCCER—Adult league play is available through the following:

- City of Los Angeles Dept. of Parks & Recreation
  Men's and Women's leagues, all levels, two seasons per year.
  818/246-5613

HIKING—The hills of Los Angeles offer miles of beautiful trails, including:

- <u>Runyon Canyon</u>
  At the end of Fuller St., North of Franklin Blvd., Hollywood
  Dogs allowed and encouraged; off-leash is permitted.
- <u>Griffith Park</u>
  At the end of Vermont Blvd., North of Los Feliz Blvd., Los Feliz
  Mountain biking and horse trails also accessible.
- <u>Malibu Creek State Park</u>
  1925 Las Virgenes Rd., Calabasas 818/880-0367
  Also offers picnic areas and some swimming in season.
- <u>Topanga State Park</u>
  20829 Entrada Rd., Topanga 310/455-2465
- <u>Will Rogers State Park</u>
  1501 Will Rogers State Park Rd., Pacific Palisades 310/454-8212
  Considered an Historic State Park due to old structures on site.

PROFESSIONAL SPORTS

Los Angeles offers a wide variety of professional sporting events, however, no professional football.

Team	Affiliation	Playing Location
Lakers	NBA	Staples Center
Clippers	NBA	Staples Center
Sparks	WNBA	Staples Center
Dodgers	MLB	Dodger Stadium
Angels	MLB	Edison Field
LA Kings	NHL	Staples Center
Mighty Ducks	NHL	The Pond at Anaheim
Avengers	XFL	Staples Center
Galaxy	MLS	LA Coliseum

MUSIC & PERFORMING ARTS

This is the entertainment capital of the world, and we have the first-class talent, performers, and venues to prove it. The following are some of Los Angeles' best bets for live performing arts:

- Geffen Playhouse 310/208-5454
  10886 LeConte Ave., Westwood
- Hollywood Bowl 323/850-2000
  2301 N. Highland Ave., Hollywood: May–Oct.
- LA Opera 213/972-7219
  Performs at Dorothy Chandler Pavilion, Downtown: Sept.–May.
- LA Philharmonic 213/972-7300
  Performs at Walt Disney Concert Hall, Downtown: Oct.–June.
- Pasadena Playhouse 626/356-7529
  39 S. El Molino, Pasadena

The city is exploding with gigs on any given night. A good place to find all of the information you are looking for, including schedules, venues, reviews, and hot tickets, is the weekly newspaper LA WEEKLY. LA WEEKLY is available free in news boxes, book stores, and coffee shops all over town; also on the web at www.laweekly.com.

MUSEUMS

From Prehistoric drawings to Picasso, you can find it in one of Los Angeles' many fine museums. The following is a list of some of the major museums in town:

- ARMAND HAMMER MUSEUM
  10889 Wilshire Blvd., Westwood 310/443-7000
- AUTRY MUSEUM OF WESTERN HERITAGE
  4700 Western Heritage Way, Griffith Park 323/667-2000
- GETTY MUSEUM
  1200 Getty Center Dr. Bel-Air 310/440-7300
- LACMA (Los Angeles County Museum of Art)
  5905 Wilshire Blvd. Mid-City 323/857-6000
- MOCA (Museum of Contemporary Art)
  250 S. Grand Ave., Downtown 213/621-2766
- MUSEUM OF TOLERANCE
  1399 Roxbury Dr. Los Angeles 310/553-9036
- NATURAL HISTORY MUSEUM
  900 Exposition Blvd. Central LA 213/763-3466

- NORTON SIMON MUSEUM
  411 W. Colorado Blvd., Pasadena 626/449-6840
- PAGE MUSEUM/LA BREA TAR PITS
  5801 Wilshire Blvd. Mid-City 323/934-7243

Additionally, the LA WEEKLY will have listings of new shows and exhibits, with critical reviews, every week.

CHARITABLE ORGANIZATIONS

Doing something to help others makes even the worst days in Los Angeles worthwhile, and opportunities to help the community abound. The following is a short list of some of the many charitable groups in town accepting volunteers:

- AIDS Education—Los Angeles Shanti
  323/962-8197
- American Cancer Society
  310/670-2650
- American Red Cross
  310/445-9900
- Habitat for Humanity
  213/975-9757
- The Los Angeles Mission
  213/893-6900; 213/629-1227
- Meals on Wheels
  310/394-7558 (West LA, Santa Monica, Malibu)
- PATH (People Assisting the Homeless)
  310/996-0034
- Elisabeth Glaser Pediatric AIDS Foundation
  310/314-1459

GETTING AWAY—PLACES TO MEDITATE

There will be times when you need to turn the noise OFF. There are some wonderful quiet places in and around Los Angeles where you can meditate, contemplate, and generally have a good think. The following is a short list:

- Center for Self Realization & Fellowship, Lake Shrine Temple
  17190 Sunset Blvd., Pacific Palisades 310/454-4114
  Called "The Lake Shrine", this is a gorgeous park-like setting with a lake, swans, ducks, koi, and otherwise beautiful silence.

- Griffith Park Observatory
  2800 E. Observatory Ave., Los Feliz 323/663-8171
  The observatory is currently closed for renovation, making it a sparsely visited and quiet destination, with great views of the city.

- Hollywood Forever Cemetery
  6000 Santa Monica Blvd., Hollywood 323/469-2392
  This is a quiet, reflective, and tasteful place, right in the middle of it all. You may find it hard to believe that it is a cemetery.

- Los Angeles Arboretum
  301 N. Baldwin Ave., Arcadia 626/821-3222
  This is one of the most beautiful gardens you will ever see. These sprawling grounds are serene and well-laid out, well-managed and maintained.

- Mulholland Drive, Los Angeles
  Drive up Cahuenga Blvd, Laurel Canyon, Coldwater, or Beverly Glen and you will hit Mulholland Drive—it stretches for miles along the mountain ridge, offering beautiful views of the city, especially at night.

- Northern Beaches: Nicholas Canyon
  33850 Pacific Coast Highway, Malibu
  Past Zuma Beach, past Trancas, way up close to the Ventura County line, tucked into the sea cliffs, are some of the most beautiful and least populous beaches on the Southern California coast.

REALLY GETTING AWAY—DAY TRIPS AND RETREATS

If you need a serious change of atmosphere, get in your car and drive. You don't have to travel far to get a breath of fresh air. The following places are no more than 140 miles from LA, but they feel a world apart, and are great areas to just simply park and explore:

- MOJAVE DESERT: Joshua Tree National Park
  74485 National Park Dr., Twentynine Palms, CA 92277. 760/367-5500
  Distance from LA: 140 miles EAST
  Travel time: 2.5 hours, approx.
  Take the 10 Freeway EAST to Highway 62. The north entrances to the park are located in the towns of Joshua Tree and Twentynine

Palms. Not far from Palm Springs, this park offers amazing desert terrain. Summers are excruciatingly hot. Best time of year to go: October—May

- <u>LAKE: Pyramid Lake State Park</u>
  43000 Pyramid Lake Rd., Gorman, CA 93243 661/295-1245
  Distance from LA: 65 miles
  Travel time: 1.5 hours, approx.
  Take the 5 freeway NORTH to exit 191, Vista del Lago Road. This exit connects to the Pyramid Lake reservoir. This is a 1,300 acre park, featuring camping, fishing, wilderness trails, boating and water sports. It snows occasionally in winter in this area (Frazier Park/Cajon Pass), making for beautiful scenery.
  Best time of year to go: April—November

- <u>BEACH: Santa Barbara, California</u>
  Distance from LA: 90 miles
  Travel Time: 2 hours, approx.
  Take the 101 Freeway NORTH, all the way to Garden Street/Laguna Street exit in Santa Barbara. There you will find a relaxed, friendly environment with a lively but laid-back cultural scene to enjoy. This is a great year-round destination.

- <u>MOUNTAINS: Lake Arrowhead</u>
  Distance from LA: 100 miles
  Travel time: 2.5 hours, approx.
  Take the 10 Freeway EAST to the 215 Freeway NORTH toward Barstow/San Bernardino. Merge onto the 259 Freeway NORTH: "MTN RESORTS". Take Highway 30 EAST to the WATERMAN/HIGHWAY 18 exit. Make a LEFT on N. Waterman/Hwy 18, until HWY 173. Make a LEFT on Hwy 173. Lake Arrowhead is a beautiful mountain destination, close to Los Angeles, with wonderful scenery, fishing and boating on the lake, and pine-mountain breezes: a great change of pace. It snows here in winter, and cabin rentals are quite affordable. This is another great year-round destination.

RELIGION

The best-kept secret in town is the religious life of Angelenos. While there are some who would publicly scoff at the idea of going to services, many, many more quietly attend. Nourishing your spiritual side is important in this competitive and stressful environment. An hour spent finding your center is never a waste of time.

There are churches, synagogues, and temples all over town, representing almost every spiritual practice and theology. You might ask your current pastor, rabbi, mullah or other religious leader for guidance in finding a place of worship in Los Angeles that resembles the one with which you are already familiar. That said, kick the tires and experiment. Most houses of worship here are exceedingly gracious and friendly to visitors, even if you have never attended a service of their kind, ever.

Even if you are a non-religious person, you may benefit from the experience. The music in churches, temples and synagogues is usually quite good, given the talent pool in Los Angeles. Going to services can be an uplifting change of pace, no matter how religious you are.

CONTINUING EDUCATION

You can learn to drive, cook, sculpt, print photographs, write sonnets, calculate your taxes, and map the human genome—all in your backyard through continuing education. These courses could be useful in whatever you decide to pursue, enriching your experience. The following are some schools that offer continuing and/or enhancement coursework:

- Los Angeles City College (LACC)
  323/953-4000
- Pasadena City College
  626/585-7123
- Santa Monica College (SMCC)
  310/434-4000
- UCLA Extension
  310/825-9971
- University of Judaism
  310/476-9777
- The Groundlings (comedy and improv school)
  323/934-9700
- BANG (comedy and improv school)
  323/653-6886

OTHER CULTURAL ENRICHMENT

Sometimes, in the course of studying for an interview, or simply in pursuit of a night in front of the TV, you might need an obscure book, video, or piece of music. Where to find it, quickly, in Los Angeles? The following is a list of some of our finest dealers in hard-to-find material:

Books:

Book Soup	310/659-3110	8818 W Sunset Blvd., West Hollywood
Dutton's Books	310/476-6263	11975 San Vicente Blvd., Brentwood
Dutton's Books	818/769-3866	5146 Laurel Canyon Blvd., No. Hollywood
Dutton's Books	818/840-8003	3806 W Magnolia Blvd., Burbank
Midnight Special	310/393-2923	3rd Street Promenade at Santa Monica Blvd.
Samuel French	323/876-0570	7623 W Sunset Blvd., Hollywood

Video:

20/20 Video	310/551-2020	6161 W Pico Blvd., Mid City
20/20 Video	323/467-2020	5420 W Sunset Blvd., Hollywood
20/20 Video	323/656-2300	8208 Santa Monica Blvd., West Hollywood
20/20 Video	323/957-2020	7064 W Sunset Blvd., Hollywood
Odyssey Video	310/477-2523	11910 Wilshire Blvd., Brentwood
Odyssey Video	818/769-2001	4810 Vineland Ave., No. Hollywood
Rocket Video	323/965-1100	726 N La Brea Ave., Hollywood
Vidiots Video	310/392-8508	302 Pico Blvd., Santa Monica

Music:

Amoeba Music	323/245-6400	6400 W Sunset Blvd., Hollywood
Aron's Record Shop	323/469-4700	1150 N Highland Ave., Hollywood
Penny Lane	310/208-5611	10914 Kinross Ave., Westwood
Penny Lane	818/566-7401	212 E Orange Grove Ave., Burbank

With all of these extracurricular activities at your disposal, you have no excuse for getting lost in your work. Stay balanced, and enjoy all of the fun cultural and educational possibilities in front of you.

INTERVIEW

Subject: Mark Anthony Little
1st Assistant Director
Credits: ***Coach Carter*, *American Wedding***

Hometown: Los Angeles, CA

Topic: Extracurricular Fun

Where did you go to school/what did you study?

Santa Monica City College, UCLA, Art Center of Design. I studied business as a minor and was debating on going into Medicine or Architecture (a long story).

When did you decide you wanted to get into entertainment?

I began managing an International Courier company in Los Angeles and wanted to start my own company. I started a smaller niche courier service in Los Angeles and although it was lucrative, It wasn't what I wanted to spend the rest of my life doing. I decided to sell and give myself a year to figure out what I was going to get into. The entertainment business always intrigued me, but for a guy with no connections I never took a career in this field as a serious reality for mere mortals.

Describe your first living situation (away from home, after school, as an independent person):

I moved out of my parents' home at 18 years of age. My girlfriend (now, wife) and I shared one car and a single apartment in Los Feliz while working my way through school.

What was your first job in this business (How old were you, how did you get it)?

One day my wife spotted an ad in the Hollywood reporter. The Ad read Film Director seeks assistant, learn the business, wend your way in, NO PAY. Perfect. I contacted, interviewed and was offered (Ha) the job (Double Ha). This was the perfect thing for me, no commitment, and because of the lack of pay, no rules, so to speak. I did the normal mundane errands to and from the studio and agency. I never stopped asking questions and helping out as much as possible. This job lasted only a few weeks because the director's film fell through. He asked me if I ever wanted to work on a set. "Of course," I answered. I was one of five additional PA/interns hired on a low budget independent film. I recall the chaos and unorganized nature of things. I also recall the attitude and general moaning and griping of the AD's on the set doing fairly basic timekeeping (Later I found out this was a production report). My questioning never stopped. I offered to help the Art department, the grip department, the camera department, and the AD's. I actually became an additional 2nd AD on the film.

How stressful was it (and was the stress a surprise)?

To me this wasn't stressful at all. After running a company and being in the "real" job market, I felt like I was in a paid apprenticeship program where the sky was the limit and there were no set rules.

How did you make the jump from that first job to being a 1st AD, to Director, then to Producer?

I made it a point to stress to people that I wanted to move up, to learn more and backed it up with action. I had to do smaller projects at first as a first AD until people knew and trusted me on larger films. I directed smaller things like Public Service Announcements and handled myself as a director's confidant to gain the trust of the producers. The Producing jobs were something that I fell into and enjoy doing.

I know you are a cycling enthusiast, and that you play the bass & the piano regularly. In addition to these outlets, how do you unwind after work?

Lots of sleep, not alcohol. I think that having a stable home base gives me an automatic change of focus.

How did you cultivate the ability to leave your work "at work"—that is to say, to not take the stress home with you?

Sometimes it is impossible, and being a first AD or Producer sometimes feels like a 24 hour job. I try to make sure as many bases are covered in the first place. I don't close myself off and try to stay a cell phone away. At least I can still be mobile. I try not to take any of it personally, but for me it is very difficult because I give a lot of myself to each job I do. I just try not to let it stress me out.

How often do you go out of town?

Usually I try a longer trip once a year and smaller trips between jobs.

Where are some of your favorite places to go (short trips)?

Place that have nothing to do with filmmaking. I love to travel. I love trying new restaurants and I love spending time with the family.

Where do you like to go (longer trips)?

N.Y., San Francisco, France, Italy, Skiing, Caribbean.

How hard is it to plan vacations in advance?

It is, but when I know I am going to wrap a show and nothing is immediately booked I book a trip. Any further is impossible.

What role does your extended family (here in LA) play in your off-time (do you see them often, touch base with them frequently, spend lots of time together, etc.)?

Sometimes the stress I feel is not being around enough. They are mostly here in Los Angeles. I try to get together as much as possible but it's not always that easy. They are finally getting used to my schedule.

What kind of an advantage, if any, do you think LA Natives have in getting started in the industry?

I am an LA native so honestly, none. I think that living in LA has its advantages but I don't think I've run into that many LA natives that often.

Any other insights?

If you do what you enjoy, you will be good at it. If it is truly what you enjoy doing, you will be successful at it. Period. Like the Italians say, "Work to live, don't live to work".

CHAPTER SIX

DATING

Prepare for a surreal experience. Dating in Los Angeles is kind of a mix between Chess, Charades, Twister, and Pin the Tail on the Donkey, only not everyone is playing on the same level. You can certainly find people of integrity in Los Angeles, though it will take some discrimination and patience to weed out the others.

Whatever you seek, you can find here in Los Angeles. We are a city of twelve million people, so no matter your persuasion—almost any taste, type, sexual preference, fetish, and ethnicity can be satisfied. It's just a matter of looking.

An individual's motivation for dating varies greatly. Dating the wrong person or making mistakes in a relationship (particularly when breaking up) can cause heavy setbacks, or in the worst case, ruin a career. Playing with hearts is playing with fire, and there are some good rules to keep in mind.

WORK RULES REDUX

In Chapter Three, you read about the rules of work conduct. Rule number eight is: Never, EVER, Date a Co-Worker While You Are Still Working Together, and it bears revisiting in this chapter. There is a strong possibility that you will break this rule at some point in your career. However, if even one person can be spared the horrendous tragedy of the "jilted-lover-in-the-workplace" scenario, this book will not be in vain.

You will spend an inordinate amount of time with your co-workers. You will get to know them well. You may get to like them, be attracted to them, dream about them. For the sake of your sanity, put the brakes on yourself before you make a move.

Consider the following hypothetical situation: Jane and Jim work at Great Big Agency A. They are both assistants to Great Big Agents. One day, Jane and Jim meet, passing in the hall, and for them, the world silently and irrevocably explodes with love. Jane tries to hide her affection for her co-worker; Jim confides to a work buddy, Newt. Jim, Jane, Newt, and a few other assistants go out for drinks a few weeks later, and no one can help but notice the sparks between Jane and Jim. At the end of the evening, when everyone has gone home, Jim walks Jane to her car and *bam* they start making out like the war's over. The next day at work is awkward. The other assistants are starting to talk. Jane and Jim decide to pursue their relationship, but strictly on the down-low, pretending (at work) that nothing happened, but seeing each other every night. Nights turn into weeks, weeks into months, and Jane becomes aggravated that she has to live a lie at work. Jim figures that one of them will have to make a change of occupation in order to continue their relationship. Jim is pretty sure it's going to be Jane. Jim and Jane talk, and neither wants to leave their job—the money, the benefits, and the connections are too good to give up. Jim tells Jane that if she is the one taking issue with having to "hide" their relationship, it should be her duty to leave the job that forces her to do so. A fight begins. Jane and Jim break up. Jane seethes with resentment at Jim for forcing the issue of leaving her job. In her anger, she fires off a ferociously-worded email regarding Jim's participation in a deal that is being made between the clients of Jim and Jane's respective bosses. Jim forwards the email to his boss. Jim's boss forwards the email to Jane's boss. Jane's boss is furious and embarrassed, and calls Jane to the mat for her unprofessional comments. Jane loses it, and spills the beans about her relationship with Jim. Knowing she needs time apart from Jim to heal, Jane quits her job.

Love can make you crazy. When you become involved with someone intimately, you begin to see the primordial emotional pulp churning inside of them. The trust required for this type of soul-baring is usually not given readily, and the rest of the world is not aware of the secrets and the knowledge (of this person) you possess. In the work environment, this secret knowledge becomes ever more powerful. The person's motivations may become clearer, and they may feel more vulnerable as a result of you being "in on" their secret emotional life. Any perceived breach of the trust will be an issue. Any personal issue will bleed over into the work place. Any relationship strife will follow you to work in the morning and sit with you all day. God forbid you should end a relationship with a co-worker and still keep your job. There is no escape from the situation, even if you have diligently kept it a secret. It is almost guaranteed that, after a bad breakup, one of you will leave your job; it will be too much to bear.

To avoid this tragedy in the first place, wait until your job is over, or until your co-worker (or you) has moved to another office, location, or division. Wait until wrap, if you are in production. Many relationships begin at wrap parties—a fine reward for being patient.

HOLLYWOOD DATING 101

No matter how smitten you are with your new love interest, THE GUIDELINES FOR INDUSTRY DATING ARE A LITTLE BIT DIFFERENT. The Petri dish of Los Angeles has cultivated some scenarios you should know about, and their potential impact on your happiness and career.

1) DATING "UP"

   Dating your professional superiors, former employers, or people with higher social or professional standing than you. This can be a dangerous game, but many men and women are attracted to people in positions of power.

   PROS:

   a) You could benefit greatly by meeting loads of interesting new people, including potential job contacts. You could be regarded as "hot property" professionally because of your association with your boy/girlfriend.
   b) You can be intellectually challenged and learn a lot from someone who has more experience and greater exposure to the industry than you have.
   c) You can experience financial security vicariously by spending time with someone who really rakes in the dough.

   CONS:

   a) While a formidable aphrodisiac, their power and influence may sink you in the end when the relationship is over.
   b) You could end up never being hired again by this person, or at worst, you could be black-balled in your professional environment. Consider the character of the person you are dating. Avoid vindictive, megalomaniacal types.
   c) You could go broke, paying for expensive dates with someone in a different financial league.

2) DATING "DOWN"

   Dating those for whom you represent an authority figure, former employees, or those with lower social or professional standing than you. This can be tricky, as well.

PROS:

a) This can be a tremendously flattering dynamic for the perceived authority figure—a big ego boost to be regarded as "better than".
b) As the perceived authority figure, dating down can make you feel useful, accomplished, and powerful, inasmuch as you can share your knowledge and experience of the industry, and give sound advice. You may also be in a position to afford career help to your boyfriend/girlfriend.
c) You can meet potential job contacts and expand your base of business associates and potential employees.

CONS:

a) You may be *expected* to help your new boyfriend/girlfriend get a leg up in the industry.
b) Due to your power or influence, you may be accused of favoritism or nepotism by offering your help to your boyfriend/girlfriend.
c) You may find that in the end you are incompatible, due to the fact that you are in different stages of your lives—quick evidence of this is that you may end up paying for everything, or the boyfriend/girlfriend moves into *your* house, rather than finding a mutually-paid-for home together, and so on.

3) <u>DATING CELEBRITIES/ACTORS</u>
When you are NOT an actor. God help you; this is an important one.

PROS:

a) Exposure to Hollywood's A-list adventure—fancy parties, glamorous premieres, talented people, all-access passes behind the velvet ropes.
b) You may achieve personal celebrity tied to the celebrity actor/actress you are dating—this is another form of "dating up", but it is done in public, and you may find that you become known for dating this person…and rich, when you publish your memoirs.
c) You may find that you are more "professionally appreciated" for the fact that you are linked to a celebrity. You may work more, and get paid more, because you are perceived to be part of the "in" crowd.

CONS:

a) Paparazzi, stalkers, starfuckers, autograph-seekers, and star-struck fans will be something YOU have to deal with by virtue of your relationship, and your boyfriend/girlfriend's celebrity. While it may have nothing to do with you, you may really resent it when you realize you can't go pick up a hamburger at McDonalds without your boyfriend/girlfriend being assaulted by fans in the parking lot.
b) Find me a successful actor who had a happy childhood, and I will give you five million d-…okay maybe fifty cents, but the point remains that actors get into the business for very specific reasons. Many actors are haunted by personal demons that, while troubling in real-life, make them riveting to watch on screen. Certainly, it is unfair to generalize. However, considering the life an actor leads—rejection or success based not only on their talent but their *looks*—the business can take a tremendous toll on even the most well-adjusted actor's ego. You might find yourself consistently positioned as the steady one, the rock, in the relationship.
c) Living in a fishbowl. Everyone will know (or think they know) what is going on in your relationship. "How was the trip to Fiji?" or "I saw you on TV at the movie premiere" is nothing compared to post-break-up "What went wrong?!" or "Why did that creep cheat on you?!". Say good-bye to your privacy.

4) DATING NON-INDUSTRY TYPES

There are people who live in Los Angeles who have nothing to do with the entertainment industry. Can you believe it? How do you find them—through friends, family, extra-curricular activities, or through one of the many web-based dating services that thrive in Los Angeles, including: www.match.com, www.eHarmony.com, www.lavalife.com, and yahoo personals.

PROS:

a) Refreshing change of pace. Here is someone who has something to bring to the table other than box office statistics or production war stories. Their non-industry insight into life can prove tremendously grounding and stimulating.
b) You can gain access to new non-industry friends who share your extracurricular interests. It is very healthy to have outside friends, with varied interests and perspectives.

c) You can vicariously experience a normal, stable life by spending time with someone who has a 9-to-5, steady, regular job, and can make plans months in advance.

CONS:

a) It is a difficult thing to explain life in the film industry to someone who isn't part of it. Your partner may tire of your work schedule (long hours, six-day weeks, location work), and your inability to make plans months in advance. Intellectually, he or she may understand it, but your being gone night after night, or day after day if you go on location, can take its toll on the relationship. Conversely, your lack of steady work may cause your partner frustration because he or she wants security.

b) People who work well in the entertainment industry are go-getters—dynamic, bright people with a lot of energy. Not every other profession demands these qualities, thus you may become bored with your non-industry boyfriend/girlfriend after a time, or you may feel that the two of you are not on the same wavelength. Whether you find a non-industry person exhilarating or boring is a personal choice you will have to make on an individual basis.

c) You may find that the goals you have set forward for yourself are incompatible with your boyfriend/girlfriend's. It doesn't take a non-industry person to provide for this type of conflict, but if your non-industry boyfriend or girlfriend wants to move back home to Omaha after you get married to raise kids, kiss your entertainment industry career goodbye.

DATING WANNABES & ESSENCE SUCKERS

You will inevitably run into people who want to be associated with you for the wrong reasons. Or, you may find yourself involved with people whom you later realize were mistakes-in-the-making.

1) PLEASE TAKE CARE OF ME

You may recognize this helpless character looking for a meal ticket, the gold digger, the wannabe. While images of breathless, rain-streaked vixens may come to mind, these sad folks are not always women. There are a lot of "helpless opportunists" in Los Angeles, and as much as we Angelenos may want to deny their existence, you need to recognize them before they get their claws in you. These are people who, in their own minds, are used-up, exhausted, beyond career rehabilitation, and have abandoned their dreams. They have given up on this cruel world, and want you to take care of them. Some of them are very attractive, and have powerful wiles. They are a dime a dozen here in Hollywood. Steer very very clear of this type.

2) THE PLAYER: WHAT WAS YOUR NAME AGAIN?
This is the charismatic alley cat, the three-week-maximum relationship, the essence sucker. Once the player has squeezed what s/he wanted from you, you are yesterday's news. The Los Angeles player is particularly insidious because he or she may come disguised in a friendly or familiar face, have a good job, and may look like a decent, respectable person. If you are suspicious, you might want to ask around about the new man/woman in your life to see if they have the "player" reputation before you become their next victim.

WHY IS IT SO WEIRD?

Everyone comes to Los Angeles with their own goals, dreams, and agendas. This is the land of dreamchasers. Often, people are so singularly focused that when they encounter something that threatens their ultimate goals (fame, fortune, and career success) they run for the hills—as if a relationship would strip them of their ability to attain their goals and achieve their best work. You will find many people here who are afraid to commit, in part because they haven't achieved what they set out to do (and thus feel "not ready" for commitment), and in part because commitment threatens an individual's freedom (to find a better partner, take a job out of town, and so forth).

It is important to keep perspective and to realize that a good romantic relationship can strengthen you as a person, thereby enhancing your career. When you are happy, everything in life is better, including work. Try not to get discouraged at the staggering number of freaks and knuckleheads in the dating world of Los Angeles. Look at the big picture, and remember that when the time is right, it will happen for you.

YOU FOUND A GOOD ONE—NOW WHAT?

Once you do get into a serious relationship, you may be asked to reevaluate your goals and plans for the future. This is the turning point in many Hollywood relationships. Do you want to get married? Do you want to have children? If so, how will you raise them? Where will you live? There is always compromise in a relationship, and maintaining balance is sometimes a challenge in this fast-paced environment.

There are ways to keep it together during the long hours of work, and/or months on location. It is important to make a commitment to your partner that you will spend time together, no matter what—whether you are on location, or just working crazy hours. There is always a compromise. Most productions welcome spouses at lunchtime—sharing a meal together and talking for a half-hour can do wonders for a relationship under the strain of a production schedule. Visiting on weekends while on location is a great idea—make the effort, even if it is a lot of work. In the end, a good relationship will enrich your life and widen your scope of sensitivity. With a little effort, and healthy compromise, it *is* possible to foster a love relationship while working your way to success in the entertainment field.

INTERVIEW

Subject: Denise Wingate
Costume Designer
Credits include: ***Wedding Crashers, Radio, She's All That, Melrose Place***

Hometown: San Fernando, CA
Moved back to LA: 1989

Topic: Keeping Relationships Alive

How did you get started in this business?

As a punk rock teen growing up in the Valley, all of my clothes were from thrift stores. When I was 16, my first job was at a clothing store on Melrose (before it was "Melrose" And WAY before I designed *Melrose Place*). When I turned 18 I moved to New York without knowing anyone and worked at clothing store on the Upper West side. I started assisting stylists doing mostly catalogue shoots and took night courses in Costume Design at John Parsons School of Design. I soon began working all of the time and eventually landed back in LA assisting a Costume Designer on a Tony Scott film starring Kevin Costner. I've been working non-stop ever since. I designed my first television show at the age of 24 and haven't looked back.

How long were you a single woman in this business before you met your husband?

I was a single woman until I met my husband when I was 29. I dated quite a bit, and am happy to say that I am still great friends with all of my exes.

What was that like, being single here, working in this world (Was it weird? How did it make you feel?)?

No, I always had a great time being single. I had a pretty busy social life, even when I was working. I never had any intention of getting married or having kids. When I met my future husband though, we just clicked immediately and we both knew that it was meant to be.

Under what circumstances did you meet your husband?

We actually had been acquaintances for 2 years before we started dating. We met at a friend's restaurant opening. He was sitting at a table with mutual friends. We would run into each other once in a while at either a club or an art gallery opening and kept exchanging numbers but never got together. He even called me to work on one of his films but I wasn't available. Finally we met one day for lunch, realized how much we had in common, and have been together ever since.

How long did you date before you were married?

We bought an amazing house together 6 months after we started dating (He had never even lived with a woman so it was a huge commitment on his part.) He proposed on our 1 year anniversary November 7th, we were married exactly one year later on November 7th and our child was conceived on November 7th on our 2nd anniversary!

When you were dating, how hard was it to see each other and to make time together (with production schedules)?

Our first year of marriage we were apart for 8 months due to location shoots.

After you were married, how did you re-prioritize your lives to allow more time together?

We both are really supportive of each others careers; we only re-prioritized our lives once our son was born. Now when one of us works, the other takes time off (we still have never worked together).

What concessions do you make together that help keep the relationship running smoothly?

The hardest thing is the hours. We're both so exhausted when we're working and you have to have the energy to keep up with a toddler when you come home.

Do you think the fact that both you and your husband work in production makes it easier or harder on the relationship?

Easier. We are very understanding and supportive…even when he was in production when I gave birth. He was there for the delivery but left for Australia weeks after the baby was born. When our son was only a year old I had to go on location for 3 months in the South. Not many men would stop working to take care of a one year old. My husband is amazing.

Now that you have a child, how have your priorities (related to work) changed?

Yes, you can't be as selfish. It's not about me or my husband any more, it's all about our son, and everything we do is based on his needs.

Anything else you'd like to add?

Just that the only way a woman can "have it all" is if they have a partner who supports and helps them. I say the same thing about the films I do. You're only as good as your crew!!!!

CHAPTER SEVEN

SUCCESS, STEP ONE

The first peak in your entertainment career is always the most exhilarating. This is the point where you've achieved the first of your goals—you've sold your first pitch, landed your first movie, booked your first big client. That's success, right? Yes, but be careful. Don't trick yourself into believing that you can stop working toward your goals.

The time following the first success is the time to really kick ass and deliver. The proof is in the pudding, friends, and if you do not produce fantastic results with your first success, it will not have been much of a success. Above all, this is not the time to gloat. There are hundreds of stories of first successes that are never fully realized. Your pitch could turn into a script that is forever lost in turnaround. Your screenplay, sold for half a million dollars, could languish on the shelf and never be made. Your first movie could get shut down and never released. Your big client could pack up and leave. Nothing, especially success, is permanent here in Hollywood. Keep it in perspective—be encouraged but not arrogant. Realize that a successful career is not so much a series of achievements, but the continuing *process* of achieving.

This is a time to look for an agent or manager, set new goals, join a union (if applicable), and to start actively managing your money. Hold on to your hat; things will change rapidly, and you may not have time to catch up.

AGENTS AND MANAGERS

There are agents who represent writers, directors, (actors) and producers. These agents are called "above the line" agents. What that means is that the cost of compensating those positions does not come out of the production budget of the project. The cost of the script, rewrites, director's fees, (actor's fees), producer's fees—all of those expenses are separate from the actual money it costs to shoot, process, and edit the film itself. "Below the line" agents represent directors of photography, editors, production designers, costume designers, assistant directors and composers. These artisans are paid with the money from the actual production budget.

The rule of thumb is that, to get representation as a writer, director, producer, director of photography, editor, production designer, costume designer, assistant director, or composer, you have to have worked on projects that people recognize as *yours*, whether through actually seeing the projects, or through looking at your portfolio/reel. You should have a body of work that provides you with a definable "style"—a way to describe you. Most agents keep a good ear to the ground for emerging talent. You may, at some point, be pursued by an agent based on your body of work, but usually in the beginning, you must approach them first.

Almost every agency in town represents clients in the two categories. Additionally, you will find individuals who have their own management companies representing people in the "above" and "below" the line categories. The difference between agents and managers is that agents are supposed to negotiate and deal with your immediate work prospects, including setting up meetings, selling your scripts, "packaging" (putting together the entire creative team for the project), negotiating licensee/ancillary marketing and soundtrack contracts, negotiating fine points in the contract (box credit, paid ads, profit participation), and following up to ensure that all contract obligations are being fulfilled. Managers are more concerned, generally, with the big-picture of your career as a whole, serving to guide an individual, steering them not only into job opportunities, but into collaborative alliances. Many "below the line" managers perform both managerial and agent duties. There are also many entertainment lawyers who can negotiate and follow up with contracts, performing these duties for a one-time fee, or a percentage on your gross income (on a project-by project basis).

There are many important considerations to be made when signing with an agent or manager.

1) <u>Prestige of the agency: client base</u>
   Some people value this more than they should. A great big top-shelf agency certainly adds a sense of legitimacy to your resume. The large client base can be a Godsend when packaging creative teams for a project. However, you may find yourself lost in the shuffle at a big

agency. They may handle too many clients to be able to service you effectively. They may not have time to return your phone calls or to follow up on your leads. It is up to you to decide whether a big name or attentive service is going to be more useful to you in the end.

2) How well do they understand you?
A good agent or manager will understand you as an artist and as a business person. You need to ensure that they know the kinds of projects you are looking for, how much you want to be paid, and your professional goals. Your agency should know your personality and your work well enough so that can they can choose projects for which you are perfectly suited. If your agency has different ideas and agendas about your career that they are pushing without your permission or knowledge, drop them immediately. You need someone who respects and understands you in order to fulfill your goals.

3) What is their reputation in the business?
Ask around before you sign with an agency. Ask production managers how quickly their phone calls are returned, whether or not they are treated respectfully in contract negotiations, and how thorough the agents' dealings are. Ask clients of the agency how they like their agent. This is a small town, and you can get honest answers if you ask the right people the right questions. Do your homework before you sign any papers. Agents and managers represent you not only as a business entity, but as a person.

When shopping around for agents, you should ask yourself, and the agent, some important questions. How do they respond to your work? What kinds of clients, personality types, do they represent? Do you feel "at home" in their client list? Is their scope of representation broad enough to allow them access to projects when YOU need access to them? What kinds of career moves have their clients made *subsequent* to their signing with the agent in question? Who are the agent's associates? How long do they want you to commit in an initial contract? Under what circumstances can they, or you, break the contract? Ask these questions as you begin to meet agents—you may be surprised at the variety of answers you receive.

Generally speaking, agents (or agencies) take 10% (regulated by state law) of the pre-tax GROSS of your pay as commission, whether they got you the job or not. Managers usually take 15% (not regulated) of the pre-tax GROSS pay, whether or not they got you the job (but negotiable depending on where one is at in their career and how much involvement the Manager expects). Ten percent? Fifteen percent? This seems like a lot of money, and it is, when you break it down. For every $1000 per week you are paid, $100 of it goes to your agent; about $320 goes to taxes. You come home with $580 for every $1000 you make, and the tax ratio cuts deeper, the more you make. However, all agent's or manager's fees are tax-deductible. ALL of the fees, all of the commissions, fall into the category of "business expense" when figuring your itemized deductions.

NEGOTIATING A GOOD DEAL

With the help of your agent, manager and/or lawyer, you can hit the jackpot financially in this business. You can also set precedent for better contracts and more perks in future negotiations. In drawing up a contract, there are several points to consider:

1) Advances: how much money you will be paid to develop a project or hold you for an upcoming project. If it is an advance, it will be deducted from future earnings. Should it be a retainer, then that fee will be in addition to the negotiated salary.
2) Immediate compensation: how much money you will be paid during pre-production and production—in a lump sum or weekly salary.
3) Days worked per week, and compensation for overtime: most union shows will shoot five days per week. Location shows sometimes shoot six days per week. What happens when you are forced to work a sixth or seventh consecutive day, wrapping or prepping, out of necessity? What if you must work on a holiday? Traveling counts as a work day—you get paid for that, too. Your agent can clarify these details.
4) Workman's comp, errors and omissions, visas, general liability: your agent will put clauses in your contract that cover the "obvious" potential mishaps regarding your work—if you get injured on the job, production will be liable for your medical costs; if they spell your name wrong in the credits, what they will do to rectify it; if you are working out of the country, the employer will supply you with a work visa; and anything else that is not specifically set forward in the contract.
5) Pay or Play: a clause of this kind in your contract means that you will be paid the negotiated salary, no matter what. Even if the project is shelved forever, your contract will be paid out. Pay or play deals can be contingent upon force majeure (an act of God or similar catastrophe that shuts down production)-"Pay or Play" deals mean you are paid in full for the duration of work you were promised, no matter

what, as opposed to "Run of Show" deals, which mean you are paid for as long as they have money, as long as the show keeps going, irrespective of what they initially told you.

6) Compensation for re-shoots and/or additional photography: Your agent can negotiate your pay scale for re-shoots, or additional photography, also stipulating that you be given first right of refusal to participate in re-shoots if you are on another project. Meaning: they have to offer you the job FIRST before they farm the work out to anyone else.
7) Deferred compensation: how much money you will be owed when the project turns a profit. You will be in line for pay behind investors, then the order (of payment) is producers, directors, writers, actors, and below-the-line. Your position of payout is negotiable and usually comes before profit (point) participants.
8) Profit participation: how much money you will make proportional to the profit of the film. These are sometimes referred to as "points"—if you have 1 point on the gross revenue of the film, you will make 1 dollar for every 100 dollars of profit earned by the film, after the initial investment is repaid with guaranteed return and perhaps deferrals. Oftentimes profit participation has a cap, a specific dollar limit, for below-the-line talent.
9) Residuals: this is a negotiated contract point that works like profit participation. You profit as the *project* profits. Depending on your deal, let's say the project makes 1 million dollars in profit when it is initially picked up by a distributor. Your first residual cut would be (let's say, for example) .25% (one-fourth of one percent) of that million dollars. The project then goes on to make more money as it is sold to foreign markets, and then to DVD and video. You make more money as the project profits. Some unions (including the DGA, SAG and WGA) require residuals contractually for their members. Residuals are commonly seen in television contracts, as a clause used when shows go into syndication.
10) Sequels: if you are involved in a project that could potentially franchise (have sequels and/or spinoffs), you can negotiate participation in development, producership, "created by" credit, or residuals/profit participation for the project.
11) Credit placement: where your credit appears, in any form, in relation to the project. This is a carefully negotiated contract point. "Favored nations" clauses in contracts help to ensure equality in credit representation, so that every department head gets a single-card credit in the opening credit roll of a film. "Box Credit" or "Paid Advertising

Credit"—where your name appears on the cover of the DVD or video box, newspaper, billboards, outdoor advertising, trade papers, and one sheets, is also an important contract point. These negotiations can get as detailed as the size of font used for your credit, and the order in which it appears in the crawl.

12) Travel and lodging: Class of travel, quality of lodging, and amount of "per diem". This can also be union-mandated, but not everyone flies coach or has to share a room, my friends. You can negotiate much more, even additional airline tickets for immediate family, (companion and/or children) should you be on location for more than one month. Per Diem is the amount of cash given to you while on location to cover your daily living expenses (like meals, taxis, and so forth). This is all negotiated up front. The amount of per diem you receive should be in line with other like-position employees, and should be based on the cost of living or expenses in the location, and can include car rentals or car allowance.
13) Reimbursements: How much, and for what, will you be reimbursed? This category would cover out-of-pocket expenses like cell phones, kit rental (meaning equipment or supplies you own, that you bring to work), computer rental, mileage, gas, internet service, and meals.
14) Advertising: Where will your name appear in any advertising related to the project? Will it appear on ads larger than 3" by 5" in major newspapers? Which newspapers? Newspapers usually included are: Los Angeles Times, New York Times, Daily Variety, and the Hollywood Reporter. What about magazine and television ads? Television ad credit is difficult to obtain for below-the-line talent and such TV ads are considered "trailers". While the credit may appear, it is not necessarily contractual.
15) Ancillary merchandise: action figures, Halloween costumes, video games, licensed merchandise. If you have created anything uniquely for a film, it is usually "owned" by the producers or producing entity. You can, however, create a rider in your contract to provide you with compensation for merchandise sales based on your design or creation.
16) Color timing, final image assessment: This gives you the option to observe and comment on optical imagery and color correction or timing of the film. This is particular to Directors of Photography, Production Designers, Special Effects Creators. Given that the industry is becoming more accustomed to digital "fixing", the artists should have the opportunity to comment on visual quality of the work done with relationship to the individuals' design.

17) Soundtracks/Books: Your agent can negotiate additional compensation for any soundtrack or book "from the movie" sales of your work.
18) Copies of your work: DVDs, VHS tapes, still photographs of your work on a project can be contractually provided to you for your portfolio or reel.
19) Press junkets: You may contractually agree to appear at press junkets (day-long interviews) or at other publicity functions for the film, and be either paid for doing so, or taken care of in style (preferential hotel treatment, airfare covered, all transportation and meals paid for, etc.).
20) Perks: Anything else not covered specifically by the above, including but not limited to—type of flowers to be arranged in hotel room, level of humidity in living quarters, allowable number of guests to be flown to location by production and put up in hotels, class and grade of rental car and/or chauffeur, and so forth.

The more money you make, the more you can conceivably spend. With 10% going to your agent, 15% to your manager, publicists' fees, lawyers' fees, accountants' fees, you could see only a sliver of your gross pay. The price of doing business is high, but remember that the above fees are tax-deductible.

REALITY CHECK

While it is tremendously helpful to have an agent, they can not guarantee you work. You will continue to have to pound the pavement for your own jobs. Even if your agent does not "find" you the job, s/he will be entitled to 10% of your gross pay. This may seem at first like an unfair business setup, but consider the benefits of having an agent. An agent is there to negotiate your contract. They make the difficult phone calls you do not want to make, including calls about salary demands, perks, and credit placement. An agent serves as a buffer between you and production so that you don't have to be confrontational about things (like salary and perks) that do not directly relate to your work on the project. An agent can get you what you want, and you will not be perceived as "difficult" because you yourself did not have to fight to get it. These are big advantages, politically. A good agent lends you credibility in your field and prevents you from getting into a political bind with production, definitely worth the 10%.

SETTING NEW GOALS

With your first success comes a time for looking back on what you have done and where you have arrived because of it. If, at this juncture, you are lucky enough to cross off some of the items on your "goals" list—good for you. It's time to make some new ones.

How well did your first set of goals serve you? How hard was it to attain them? Consider your past when you make your goals for the future. If you can, look to those who have pursued similar career paths to you. At what point in their lives do you line up? Can you chart a logical trajectory from there? Look closely.

No two people have the same career trajectory. However, you can learn more about what to do and what NOT to do by looking at the examples of people who have gone before you. Read some biographies. Do your research on www.imdb.com—study the career paths of people whose careers you admire. See how they made their next move after their first big success. Think about it, and then write those goals down.

JOINING A UNION

If you are involved in an art/craft profession, or are a director, producer, or assistant director, you will at some point be thinking about joining a union. Usually, there are a number of days of sanctioned employment required to join, and a hefty initiation fee. Some shows "roll" union, meaning that they are organized by the union during the production period. Most employees automatically gain entry into the union that has organized the show, but they still have to pay the hefty initiation fees. The following are some of the unions and the departments they cover:

- Director's Guild of America (DGA)
  Covers: Directors, Assistant Directors, Second Assistant Directors, Second-second Assistant Directors, Second Unit Directors, Line Producers, Trainees.
- Writer's Guild of America (WGA)
  Covers: Writers of all kinds
- International Alliance of Stage and Theatrical Employees (IATSE)
  Including, but not limited to the following departments: Art, Camera, Craft Service, Editing, Grip, Hair, Make-up, Lighting, Production Coordinators, Script Supervisors, Sound, Special Effects, and Wardrobe.
- ASCAP
  Covers : Composers, Orchestrators, Music editors, Music Producers.
- Teamsters
  Covers: Transportation, Locations

The benefits of union membership are vast. The health coverage included with qualifying membership in any of these unions is hands-down the best in *any* industry. These unions also offer continuing education, networking, research libraries, and retirement benefits. The Motion Picture Industry Home is a well-known haven for aging industry pros, and also comes as a benefit of union membership.

MANAGING YOUR MONEY

There is one thing you need to know about personal financial health in the film industry: this is a feast-or-famine economy. You may make a lot of money on a single project, but subsequent to that boon, you may not work for a few months. The long-term effects of this cycle can be ruinous to your credit and to your relationship with money, unless you manage it very, very carefully. You may have goals to make a lot of money, but the real point in all of this is to never go broke. The "feast or famine" economy introduces a new set of criteria for managing your money, which will have you dancing to a different financial rhythm than you're accustomed to.

Some common rookie mistakes include overextending your limits with credit cards. This is the quickest way to cripple yourself with debt. When you make a large sum of money, PAY OFF your credit cards and your debt FIRST! The interest rates on your credit cards are much higher than the earned interest rates on any typical investment. Be smart about your money, and take your management of it seriously. Make your money work for you.

If you don't have a savings policy in your life already, consider developing the discipline to save money while you are earning it. Putting away even a small amount, every week, from your paycheck, into an interest-earning savings or money-market account can really come in handy. Try not to touch that money, unless you are a hair's breadth away from car repossession and/or bankruptcy. Even if you save only ten dollars per week, you will have money tucked away that you could use to contribute to your retirement fund, or to rescue your piece of $hit car from the tow yard.

If you come into a sudden financial windfall, BE SMART! Consult a financial planner for advice on what to do with your money if you realize you are in over your head. Even if you have quickly made a truckload of money, live below your means. You never know when it will dry up, or how hard you are going to be hit at tax time. Plan shrewdly for the future, and organize your finances so that you never have to be broke.

Start saving receipts for itemized deductions at tax time. Within your specific field, you may find a goldmine of allowable itemized deductions. Here are some general categories allowable for deduction in the entertainment industry:

- Cable TV
- Industry-related Magazines
- Movie tickets
- Movie Rental
- Cell phone (for business purposes)
- Pager
- Home phone (for business purposes)
- Internet Service (for business purposes)
- Mileage (when not reimbursed)
- Purchases of computers, DVD players, electronics (used in business)
- Meals (where you have discussed business)
- Agents' commission
- Postage (for business purposes)
- Charitable contributions

With all of these itemized deductions, you will need to find a Certified Public Accountant to do your taxes. Most CPAs in Los Angeles are adept at filing taxes for people in entertainment. It may cost you a few hundred dollars, but you will have the satisfaction of knowing that your taxes were done thoroughly by a professional. A good CPA can also help you to uncover new and unforeseen avenues to save on your taxes, like incorporating.

If you make over $150,000 per year, it makes sense to incorporate. When you incorporate yourself as a business, you are fully paid up front. You pay taxes *later* (either quarterly or at the end of the year) based on how much you have earned, less your business expenses (meaning agents' commission and itemized deductions). This type of accounting is more useful the more money you make, and at some point, you will need to consider the option of incorporation.

Perhaps the biggest benefit to taking care of your finances is giving yourself the freedom to choose your projects. You may not amass a mountain of wealth, but if you have enough money so that you are not forced to take any project because you *need the money*, you have realized a very important goal. Choosing your projects is in a way, controlling your destiny. Managing your money means more than dollars and cents, it means taking control of your life.

SETTING UP AN IRA

At some point, sooner rather than later, it would be wise to set up an IRA (Individual Retirement Account). This money earns tax-free interest until you retire (you can have penalty-free access to your money at age 59 ½). Regular IRA contribution limits are $2,000 per year. You can set up a ROTH IRA if you make less than $150K per year. Annual contribution limit for a Roth IRA is $3000. If you squirrel away $3000 per year, every year, you will have a nice sum of money when you turn 59 ½. If you are completely self-employed, you can set up a SEP-IRA (for Self-Employed Persons). You cannot set up a SEP-IRA if you are a member of a union or other group that provides you with 401(K) or pension benefits. Consult your CPA for advice.

DON'T BURN BRIDGES

Most importantly, when you have tasted your first success, do not burn bridges. You may feel like telling your boss to shove it in his ear, but refrain! You may or may not need your old boss again for an important connection or bit of advice. Why leave under bad circumstances if you don't have to? Realize that the fabric of Hollywood is tightly woven but fragile indeed. If you tear it, you may never be able to repair it. Transition gracefully into your new success, and give thanks and credit to the people who helped you along the way. Maintaining your success with grace will be the one thing that saves you, no matter what happens.

INTERVIEW

Subject: Todd Quinn
CFO, Endeavor Talent Agency
Clients of Endeavor include: Drew Barrymore, Adam Sandler, Ben Affleck, Michael Moore, James Cameron, McG, Brannon Braga, Dean Koontz

Hometown: Dallas, TX
Moved to LA: 1995

Topic: Financial Health

Describe how you made the decision to move to LA:

During the summer of 1995, I was working for a large audit/consulting firm in Dallas, TX, dealing with real estate partnership audits/transactions for developers and investors. Although I excelled in my field, I was bored.

A headhunter called asking if I would consider working for Disney. They were looking for individuals with education/experience similar to mine. Knowing little of Disney or Los Angeles and wanting something more in my life, my interest was piqued. I flew to Houston the following week to interview with the Disney recruiters, then on to Los Angeles the next to meet with my potential new department. I had never visited Los Angeles and flying into LAX that night, I remember the fear of the unknown in the sea of lights. What was I doing?

Three weeks later I was living in LA. Disney took care of packing my home in Dallas, shipping my car to LA, giving me a one way ticket to Burbank, and setting me up with temporary housing near the studio. I could not have asked for a simpler, more coordinated transition. But...what did I know about this industry? Absolutely nothing.

Describe that first job here:

My first job at Disney was in a group called Management Audit, part of the corporate world of Disney. I guess you could say we were the "police" or "CIA" of Disney. We would individually visit the different divisions of Disney around the studio, around the world, even visiting outside licensees of Disney merchandise. Learning about theme parks, production, licensing, film/video distribution, and any other arena usually happened in the *field* or on the plane.

After Management Audit, I took a position in the Feature Animation department managing the overhead budgets for a variety of departments such as casting, development, post production, and human resources. I learned a great deal about the industry, people within the industry and the *politics*, and budgeting/forecasting/reporting for this unique environment. I stayed with Disney for four years.

It would take an unpleasant stint as the head of finance for an emerging PR firm, then another year as the finance director for a software development/high tech company, before finding my resting spot here at Endeavor.

When/how did you become CFO of Endeavor?

In June 2001, sitting at my desk at a quickly sinking company in the decline of their segment of the high-tech/communications industry, I was searching the web and answered a blind ad for an accounting/finance position with a "Beverly Hills Talent/Literary Agency". Once again, my interest was piqued. This would give me a completely different perspective into the reason that brought me to LA…the entertainment industry.

It was months before I received a kind call from human resources at Endeavor. I had almost forgotten that I had even submitted a resume to a talent agency from this blind ad. This must have been the place…newer agency, a great group of talented partners/agents, quickly growing list of clients, lean/entrepreneurial environment.

I interviewed and became Controller. A year later, with the departure of our last CFO, I was promoted.

What kinds of clients does Endeavor represent (what kinds of positions in the industry)?

Actors, Television and Feature writers, producers, and directors.

What are your job duties?

I manage anything and everything related to the movement of money, whether it is money flowing in/out for our clients, processing payroll for the agency, acquisition/disposition of assets, budgeting, forecasting, and reporting.

How much and what kinds of money are you responsible for?

A lot. My group manages the flow of monies through the agency for our clients, we "pay the bills" for the agency, process payroll, and account for each process accordingly.

What are some of the major mistakes people in this business make in managing their money?

In my opinion…the biggest mistakes from people in general, not just people "in the business", result from lack of planning, thinking short term, living beyond one's means, not planning for the future, losing touch/connection/understanding with one's finances, and not taking advantage of investment.

Are there any steps people coming up can take to ensure their financial security?

Plan, save, invest, stay connected to the decisions regarding your finances, and avoid over-extending oneself.

Any advice in setting up an IRA or managing a 401(k)?

The biggest mistake I find with IRA/401(k) is the lack of participation, or a reduced or halt of participation during a falling market. These programs, designed for the long term, allow you to invest money for your retirement/future that you would otherwise pay in taxes. The earlier you begin taking advantage of these pre-tax savings programs, the better. I find myself teaching people not to stop their contributions, slow their contributions, or cash out of their program when they see that they've lost or are losing money. That is typical the time to keep buying (investing) at the lower rates. It becomes a game of averages.

What are the advantages/costs of having a business manager or full-time accountant?

First and foremost...stay involved and informed with your finances. However, having a business manager/full-time accountant allows people in the industry to focus on what they do best...act, write, produce, direct, costume, agent, etc. Money/investment can then be properly managed who understand your specific goals and tax situation.

Anything about your business that surprises you?

Surprises me? These days, little "surprises" me in this city and in this industry. I am always fascinated to see/experience how such a widely diverse/talented group of people come together to create art, film, and television. There is great vision in this agency.

CHAPTER EIGHT

SETBACKS

This is perhaps the most important chapter in the entire book. Why? Because setbacks, failures, mistakes are inevitable in this business. You may find yourself fired, out of work for long periods, blackballed, running out of money and living on prayer alone. Amigos, we have ALL been there. Setbacks are the one thing we in the entertainment business have in common.

DON'T PANIC

Take some solace in the fact that setbacks are never going to disappear from your life, ever. They may at first appear daunting, but they only become hurtful or devastating when you LET THEM. Take some time to look around and learn something when you face hard times. What does the situation tell you about yourself?

Let's say you were fired. You overstepped your boundaries for the last time and your boss had had it up to here. Look inside of yourself and account for your bad behavior. Try to figure out what made you behave in that manner. Work on it, and get to know yourself. The solutions begin within! Do the work! When you get into your next job, you will be ahead of the game. You can avoid the triggers for the bad behavior, do a better job, and not get fired.

Let's say you are running out of money. You have about $1000 left in your bank account, and more than $1000 in bills to pay. Folks, it's time to revisit the temping, catering, or nannying world. Above all, do NOT get yourself in debt, overextended on credit cards, in hopes of your next big break. Gambling on your career in this manner is addictive. Before you start borrowing from Peter to pay Paul, get thyself to the temp agency, catering job, or nanny agency. Do not get into the hole. You need to keep yourself financially afloat, first and foremost. Even if you don't make very much money temping, catering, or nannying, you *will* be putting a dent in your potential debt. Additionally, temping, catering, and nannying can be a real boost to a deflated ego in a time of unemployment. The fact that you can be useful, helpful, and/or feel needed can really lift your spirits. As depressing and humiliating a thought it might be (returning to temping or catering or nannying, after you have tasted success), living life without feeling useful is infinitely worse. Take care of yourself, financially and emotionally!

Most importantly, keep your head straight and your eye on the prize. Remember why you came to Hollywood and what you set out to achieve. It's time to make a new goals list; this time with a twist.

STOP—START—CONTINUE

Revisit your old goals list—the one you updated when you had your first success. Look at it carefully. What is working, and what can be abandoned? This period of "setback" is the classic *death and rebirth* motif that we encounter in life, asking us to get rid of the old to make way for the new. When evaluating your old goals list, and formulating your new list, here are some examples of questions you might ask yourself:

1) What should I STOP doing?
   Examples:
   - I should STOP working on low-budget movies that are made without care.
   - I should STOP doing rewrites for films like *Sorority Massacre 6*.
   - I should STOP taking on my bosses' personal dramas at work.
   - I should STOP trying to branch out into commercials, and stick to films.

2) What should I START doing?
   Examples:
   - I should START sending my resumes to people I don't know.
   - I should START networking again with my College Alumni Association.
   - I should START developing my own projects.
   - I should START writing my own script.

3) What should I CONTINUE to do?
   Examples:
   - I should CONTINUE to kick ass in everything I do.
   - I should CONTINUE to demand artistic excellence in the workplace.
   - I should CONTINUE to seek good projects that are well-financed.
   - I should CONTINUE to seek raw, undeveloped talent & hone it.

Write this down, and ruminate on it. Take the time to really think about your focus in the months ahead, and the changes you would like to make in your life and in your career. Be specific, and be thorough. The more you think the STOP—START—CONTINUE list through, the easier it will be to make it happen.

WHEN SETBACKS COME AT YOUR OWN HAND

You may find yourself at a crossroads in your career where your "STOP" list takes its toll on your career progress. You may find yourself out of work for months at a time, passing on project after project based on lack of time, lack of money, familiar territory, and/or content. These are your choices to make. You are in the driver's seat of your career, and you will need to make choices about which roads you take.

When you have been down "Low Budget Lane" enough times over the years, you will need to STOP going there, lest your career breaks down on the side of the road and no one can get it started again. If you take a project that is centrally located on "Low Budget Lane", you may be providing yourself with a setback of another kind: enslavement to a paycheck. This kind of enslavement sucks your creative juices and enthusiasm right out of your guts, leaving you exhausted with nothing left to give, and no time to look for other work. This is the time to choose between two setbacks. The things you choose NOT to do can help you more than the things you choose TO do. Prune your own rosebush.

The setbacks you experience at your own hand, clearing the way for your career path ahead of you, are really not setbacks. These are necessary growing pains, and no growth in this business is achieved without some modicum of pain and suffering. It is worth it.

SEEKING HELP

There may come a time, following a particularly difficult setback, where you may need to seek help from a professional. Do not let your pride get in the way of your progress! There are many talented mental health professionals in Los Angeles who specialize in things like writer's block, creative impasses, self-esteem building, and so forth. Your health insurance may even cover some of the cost. If you are running out of money, you can still talk to a counselor on a sliding-pay-scale, meaning that you pay as much as you can afford. There are a few great clinics that offer these services:

1) California Graduate Institute, Graduate School of Professional Psychology Westwood/next to UCLA
   310/208-4240

This is a mental health counseling center staffed by graduate students studying psychology. They are a sliding-scale clinic.

2) Westminster Center for Personal Development, Pasadena
626/798-0915
This is a sliding-scale mental health clinic, with many accredited counselors to help you. This clinic accepts Motion Picture Health insurance as payment.

Talking with a professional can really help to alleviate stress, and you can learn a few things about yourself in the process. The time and effort you spend getting to know your inner self and your motivations will always be worthwhile. Your new self-awareness will improve not only your career, but also the rest of your life.

CARRYING ON

You will still need to send out resumes, send out scripts, pursue all of your options, and innovate. Do not let the rejection get to you. One of the most important things you can possess at this time is faith: faith in your ultimate success in this business and faith in your purpose for being here. Learn from your mistakes, and carry on. Lick your wounds, learn your lessons and do not give up.

Continue to innovate in your field, if you can. Write a new script, figure out new avenues for developing talent, come up with a new way of shooting a scene, new lighting schematics, scenic designs—continue to stoke your creative fires. Do not let yourself get stagnant in the times when you are out of work. Push yourself creatively; force yourself to innovate.

THE SILVER LINING PRINCIPLE

The "Silver Lining Principle" is that bad news may be *opportunity* in disguise. It is a matter of perspective. You may have to work to adopt and integrate the "silver lining principle" into your thinking, but consider the following:

Anne works as a production designer, and has been out of work for two months. She is very good at her job, but has not had a "big break" yet. In the course of *one* week, Anne's boyfriend dumps her, her car is totaled in a collision, she's running out of money, and she loses two Great Big Jobs she was up for. This is bad news for Anne. She spends the following three days crying her eyes out: *why me?!* Out of the blue, Anne's agent calls with a small but sturdy independent feature. Trouble is, it shoots far, far away in a place Anne's never been. Anne is beyond frustrated: *fine, send me the script; why not?!* She meets on the project, and figures: *what the hell?!* Having nothing better to do, Anne goes, and it changes her life. She meets new friends, falls in love, and the project becomes a huge success. Anne would have never been able to experience all of this if the death of the old (the breakup with the boyfriend, the loss of the jobs) had not made way for the new.

Before you start to feel to sorry for yourself about the misery that has befallen you, think of what "rebirth" you might be readying for yourself. Try not to get too caught up in the pity party. Set aside two hours, precisely two hours, to cry your eyes out and wail so hard that the world cries with you. Then, stop it and get over yourself. There are many people in the world who have it so much worse than you. Remember the "Silver Lining Principle", and soon you may not even believe that you cried over something as wonderful as the changes taking place right in front of your eyes.

REBUILDING AND REBIRTH

In the rebuilding/rebirth process, you may get to the point where you need to give *yourself* the "Life Is Short/One Shot" Lecture detailed in Chapter One. Remind yourself of your worth, and why you are here. Good things are worth fighting for, and if you have a dream, you are obliged to pursue it.

You will need to be strong and focused. You will also need the support of your friends and family. This is the time to lean on your friends, and to really seek them out for companionship and advice. You may learn some things about yourself during these setbacks that will ultimately make you better at what you do. These are "character building" times, and though that seems like cold comfort in the face of a harsh setback, you will come to appreciate your personal gains in the long run. These setbacks and failures help to define our successes, and help us to mature as artists and as people.

INTERVIEW

Subject: Daniel Gillies
Actor
Credits: *Spider-Man 2, Trespassing, Bride and Prejudice*

Hometown: Hamilton, New Zealand
Moved to LA: 2002

Topic: Death and Rebirth Cycle

When did you start your career in New Zealand?

I landed a couple of small television roles in 1994, before training full-time at the Unitec School of Performing Arts for Screen and Theatre in Auckland, New Zealand. I graduated 2 years later. So I would say that my professional career officially began at the end of '96.

What kind of career did you have there?

In many ways New Zealand was actually my rite-of-passage/actor's struggle/self-indulgent tale of woe. Though there was arguably less competition, there was an incredibly small pool of work there, especially in early '97. Most New Zealand actors have worked in theatre, and I was no exception. I spent my first 3 years doing shows all over the place; working in every major theatre in the country, which in retrospect, I'm incredibly grateful for. Nothing conditions the actor like working in theatre. In between acting with theater companies, I wrote and directed my own play, put on shows at smaller theater venues with buddies, performed in independent features and short films for nothing and took commercial work. I had a further couple of stints as a guest star in trashy American shows shooting in New Zealand, and then I was cast as a lead in a Kiwi pilot called *Street Legal* in late '98. I went on to do 2 seasons of the show (which consumed about 7 months of the year), more trashy TV, a God-awful B-grade American flick and plays in the off-season.

The first 3 years were positively grueling. When I couldn't do acting of any kind in New Zealand, I sustained myself with a slew of occupations; I have been a barman and a waiter (obviously) at about 5 different places; I worked in radio promotions as an errand-boy, was a cleaner for 12 mechanics in an automotive repair station; I sold clothes, worked as a photo-copying guy, water-blasted the hulls of Naval vessels, washed dishes in a kitchen the width of 4 feet, worked terrifying solo-graveyard shifts in a liquor store for almost a year (I was robbed twice; offering little resistance to physical threat in each instance—I was earning 9 bucks an hour), sold bullshit jewelry from a suitcase to victims at fairs and festivals, screamed myself hoarse for 4 months—5 hours a day outside a store that sold liquidated stock...armed only with a microphone and an amplifier in main street, Auckland. I dressed as an eagle to sell pizzas.

Most of these were not "in-between" jobs. These were jobs that I carried out during performances. I think that was one of the startling things I saw when I first came to L.A. Everybody here wanted to be a star, but nobody wanted to be any good—to learn and train like a badass to become an actor. In New Zealand people wanted to act. And that meant doing anything and everything you could to do what you loved to do. Often that meant sustaining yourself with a crappy job. No one could even begin to think of themselves as a star because there was no fucking star system. Even when I became a "highly-paid" actor back home, my income was laughable compared to here and to Canada. In the United States, people do not laugh at you if you tell them you are an actor. It's beautiful. Here, you can make an incredible living: the Screen Actors Guild is a phenomenal force and there is an abundance of work.

By the time I was 25 I had a good career back in New Zealand. I was working consistently between theatre and TV, I was generating a decent income and I hadn't had to do any bullshit jobs in almost 2 years.

My heart was slowly breaking.

What do you postulate would have been your future if you stayed there?

A safe and unextraordinary plateau of guest leads and poorly written medical dramas. An ultimately miserable experience.

When and why did you decide to come to Hollywood?

I'll answer the "why" first. After a brief stay in Sydney, Australia in 2001, I was persuaded (with the last of my cash) to come and try my hand in the Canadian scene. Fortunately I was Canadian-born, which made it very simple for me to get Social Insurance numbers, etc., so before long I started washing dishes and waiting tables for a couple of places (one was Planet Hollywood, would you believe). The first refuge I found in Vancouver was the floor of an apartment the size of a box of Mini Wheats, which I shared with 7 cats. I was broke, so that suited me down to the rancid ground. Unfortunately, 2 of my feline cohorts died after consuming a loaf of cotton debris one day, so I read this as an omen to depart swiftly. Before long I was beating the feet in Vancouver, knocking on the doors of agencies. I found representation and soon I was acting in Canada. I consider myself extremely lucky, especially because S.A.G. strikes and 9-11 didn't inspire the most fertile conditions for production in Vancouver, and somehow I landed a few roles in a mini-series, a pilot and a Canadian independent. I found a space to teach technique a couple of times a week which made me happy, and also generated a little bit of an income to tide me over between roles...I was not going back to a restaurant again. So to answer the 'why' (in the most convoluted way imaginable), I found Vancouver to be as insular and delusional as Auckland and Sydney. There were a handful of casting directors who had an absolute monopoly on who was and wasn't auditioned there. Many of these people knew nothing about acting. There was an elite of about 4 actors in every category that seemed to be cast in everything. The greatest roles were always cast out of L.A., though you would wearily turn up to the obligatory cattle calls. Gratefully, I was seen by a couple of gracious casting people, with an actual vision beyond their own egos, and I was mercifully cast. But basically, I could sense myself getting comfortable and complacent again in Vancouver—which, to me, equated to nowhere fast.

When? I guess I had come to Vancouver, knowing that I would eventually make my way down here. I even thought I might spend another year in Canada before I came down to L.A. But if I was actually specific, I was in a bar talking to a dude I just met, in October 2001, who invited me to join him on a voyage to L.A. that he had chosen to make in 3 months time. It was phenomenal, because he and I barely spoke between that night at the bar and the ensuing 3 months. Also, he'd just been cast in a movie in Vancouver for which, a week before, we were both competing for the lead role, and because he'd booked the job, he felt financially comfortable making the decision to come to Los Angeles. A weird and auspicious evening. I was punched in the eye by a gangster in the bar later that night.

How hard was it for you to make that decision?

I'm not a practicing Christian, but I've heard Christians say that "the Lord is my shepherd". I don't believe I made that decision, as such. And I'm honestly not trying to be romantic, but I have always tried to pursue the things that my heart told me to. Though sometimes certain junctions pose powerfully different outcomes, I believe that I have always been shepherded and blessed enough to see what I had to do to be happy. Even if it involved trial and hardship, God was always careful to punctuate certain things. Unfortunately, sometimes his punctuation marks can look a little like black eyes and eagle costumes.

What did you tell your family and friends?

I'm going to Los Angeles.

Did you know anyone in Los Angeles before you came?

No.

How did you support yourself when you arrived?

I did not support myself. I think I arrived with around $125 in my pocket. That depleted fast.

I knew I was not leaving.

Describe your first living arrangement:

I spent the pilot season of 2001 on a couch in the living room of the assistant to my manager. I couldn't really call it a couch, either. It was 2 decrepit lounge seats that you would turn 90 degrees to face each other. And the only problem that you faced once you'd assembled this "couch" was that it was not long enough to support anyone taller than Dudley Moore.

As grateful as I am to the person who so generously looked after us, I don't even think that he would disagree that the place was a disturbing comedy.

My Canadian buddy and I managed to scrape by on Chicken of the Sea, Top Ramen and Marlboro lights. I had no cell phone and no money, so my agent in Canada actually mailed me a Canadian cell from Vancouver to use. I had no car, so my Vancouver ally and I spent whole days in his car moving from his auditions to my own.

I remember feeling happier than I had ever been during that time. I knew that I was home. I adored L.A., and embraced every aspect of our meager circumstances. As easy as other people found it to be cynical about the town, I found an unparalleled joy and excitement. Los Angeles was the home to people who dreamed and felt that their dreams were near. It was enchanting.

Fortunately, I managed to secure a few test deals during that pilot season. I took the first pilot that I booked. Minutes later, and five weeks after landing in L.A., I was on a plane to Johannesburg, South Africa.

Was there ever a low point when you thought you had made the wrong decision; did you ever regret it?

Never.

I mean, I've had tough times. I've definitely griped and bitched to my buddies when I felt beat up. But I truly believe that the decision is often made before the battle. I think many of us decided that we would do this as children.

When I returned from South Africa, I guess I figured: "Hey, I booked that pilot in no time.... How long can it take to get something else?"

What ensued was 12 months of narrow misses. Sometimes I would go in 5 or 6 times for certain things, and still not get the role. People were frightened of casting the 'unknown'. They were always gracious in acknowledging what I could do...but often felt conflicted, because of this anonymity. As a New Zealander, I could only shoot for feature leads and series regulars, which significantly slimmed the amount of auditions I could go out on. Once I even got myself a little role...but was unable to do it, because I could not obtain the appropriate work papers within a given period of time.

My money swiftly vanished, and before long it was back to the game of survival. Fortunately, I was no stranger to that world. And compared to what I had undergone in New Zealand, L.A. was a fucking cake-walk.

By the time the next pilot season rolled around, I was positively reluctant to do it again. This time I did not have a car...and (enter my self-righteous badge of honor) I did almost the entire pilot season of 2003 on the subways and buses of this fair city.

The tests did not come so generously this time.

But I never felt any regret. Defeats on your path to your love aren't even really defeats. If you have any psychology other than that, you will not prevail.

How did you find the strength to carry on?

As low as I may have fallen, it was remembering the decision to make this journey that made me happy. I did not resent the decision to walk this path because of the hardship. It was a question of courage to continue, and not strength for me. If carrying on is your only option, then you are truly at home in your destiny.

Also, I have incredible friends and people that I love here in L.A. We vent to each other when it is time to vent.

Under what circumstances did you get your big break?

I hope I'm not a boring interview, Kristin. But I really don't believe in the conventional "Big Break". To me the big break for an actor is the moment a man or woman knows that they can only be an actor. I could talk to you about Spiderman and gush about how everything turned upside-down, but it would be complete fiction to tell you that a glamorous opportunity was a break of any kind. To me the big break is often engendered in the darkest hour, the hardest place, drenched with the snot and tears of another defeat. The "Big Break" is the moment a courageous heart says to pain and adversity: "I believe in this dance I'm dancing. I'm not leaving the dance floor."

To what do you attribute your big break/rebirth process?

I really don't know. I understand that I am very blessed. I think I keep an ear open to the universe. Not as much as I should...but just enough to hear certain things occasionally.

How has your life changed since 2002?

It's a strange time. It's April, 2004.

I'm in this kind of gelatinous period where I have acquired a reputation within the industry, but it is a reputation that opens the door only so far. The hype enshrouding the couple of projects that are yet to launch later this year is enough to be able to side-step certain formalities. For example, I am able to get into rooms with directors fairly immediately; I don't have to do the preliminary auditions for projects. Occasionally, an offer for a movie even comes in...which I had never received before this year.

And yet I'm not Josh Hartnett, Leonardo DiCaprio or Colin Farrell. I'm immensely grateful that I'm not, but my name doesn't actually finance a film. Most investors in this town couldn't give a flying fuck about talent or skill. They want their bucks back, and they want 'em back fast.

I'm incredibly grateful for my experience, though. I now have money in my pocket. I have a beautiful place to live. I actually have a little momentum with a career here in the United States. My life has changed considerably. I read many, many scripts. I read many, many poor scripts. The beginning of 2002 was a baptism by fire, and my breadth of understanding of this place and how it functions expands all the time. I'm fighting a different battle now, however. I'm trying to learn patience and calm. I don't want to make stupid decisions and commit to things out of fear.

Any strategies for getting through the tough times?

For an actor "tough times" is usually the down-time, which is when we are unemployed. Granted, there are occasions when working actors are not happy, but I have found that the anxiety and frustration of unemployment can make everything that is unfortunate in your life seem a whole lot worse. Gratefully, my time in New Zealand altered all of that. By the time I was about 25, I really began to look at the "tough times" as opportunities. Now I do, even more so. These times are designed for us to use. Take up a tango, read about a chapter of history that you don't know about, learn Spanish, play the tuba...get a new fucking skill. I guarantee, sooner or later you will incorporate this into your work. Take it as a given that you will work again, and embrace the privilege of being able to work on yourself. The energy of "tough times" forges the greatest artists.

I heard many people along the way say that I would not realize my desire to become an actor and that I would not survive Los Angeles. Anyone who believes this will surely fall. No one and nothing can stop you from becoming everything that you believe you are.

Dispose of competition with others as an artist. It's a waste of time. I've witnessed many artists who gesture to various careers which "happened overnight", looking to other artists to compare themselves or to complain of the injustices of the industry. I've never understood that psychology. I'm not an "overnighter" and I'm fucking pleased I'm not. Those careers rarely have any longevity. I feel terrible for these gorgeous-looking children who are suddenly told that they are actors; breast-fed on hype and the greed of the people that represent them. The "overnighter" almost never hones their craft, or works to develop their skill as an actor other than learning to smoke a cool cigarette and parallel-park a HUM-V. As time went by I realized just how fortunate I am that I have had all of my own experiences of survival—both as an actor and as a man—before achieving anything substantial in the United States. I would surely not be the kind of actor that I am now, without the grace of those hardships. Although I've never played the sport in my life, a buddy of mine and I always note the congruencies of golf and acting. Yes, there are other people playing the game...but ultimately, it's just you and the ball; a test of your focus, power, patience and skill. The only competition is with yourself.

Always let the greatest criticism of anything you do be your own. It's simple to find fault, especially with an actor's performance. I admit—I do it all the time. It requires insight and imagination to discern what someone's strengths are, especially if they are performing in a piece of shit. Whenever you do something, be mindful of what in your eyes needs to change, and what feels right. Surround yourself with good people, people who will not bullshit you to massage your ego or bullshit you to empower themselves. It can become quite destructive when an actor places someone else's ideas before their own; it can obliterate one's confidence. More destructive still, is the danger of the honey-dipped words of sycophants and charlatans. Discern who is and who is not telling you what you want to hear. When an actor reaches a certain level in this town, that seductive hand will always come. Your heart will always tell you what the truth is.

Anything else?

Find good people. Surround yourself with good people. There are great people in this town...dreamers like yourself...you just have to look. They will be your greatest solace from the storm. Find people who want nothing from you other than to be friends with you. Find passionate people that lift and inspire you. I am incredibly blessed, in this respect.

CHAPTER NINE

WATCHING YOUR FRIENDS SUCCEED

No two people have the same career trajectory. Things happen for us in our careers when the time is right. It can be frustrating to watch your friends succeed, but consider the following scenario:

Person "A" (we'll call him Andy) and Person "B" (we'll call him Bill) are best friends from high school. Andy and Bill dreamed of being screenwriters their entire lives, and are now 27 years old. Andy has been living in Los Angeles since he graduated college, at which time he won a screenwriting competition and a large cash prize. Andy has since sold one script for low-six-figures that has never been produced, and sold one TV pilot pitch a year ago that never went to series. Andy writes every day. Bill stayed in their hometown, writing and producing no-budget community theater for five years. At 27, Bill moved to Los Angeles to pursue his dream, and within six months sold a spec script to Great Big Studio A for a million dollars. Two months later, Bill pitched a project to Celebrity Production Company B, and it sold for mid-six-figures. A month went by, and Bill was approached by Great Big Studio Executive X to "doctor" a major action movie for Great Big Studio A. CUT TO: Andy looking on in horror, slack-jawed at the sudden stroke of luck visited on his friend Bill.

WHAT TO DO?

The above scenario is not at all uncommon in Hollywood. Not everyone is on the same time-table here. Some people toil for years in obscurity, only to one day suddenly catch a break and be touted as the best "new" talent in the industry! If you are lucky enough to witness massive success of your friends, by all means <u>celebrate it</u>.

It may be hard to celebrate when you are silently suppressing a jealous rage that would wipe out half the city. If you really are freaked out, and can not bring yourself to be happy for your friend, excuse yourself for a day or two. Step back and look objectively at the situation from all sides. Jealousy is a destructive state of being that will do nothing but damage you and your relationship with your friend. Find a place in your heart where you can celebrate your friend's success. Adjust your attitude.

Your friends are your mirrors in life, and the people who surround you say a lot about where you are in life. If your friends suddenly become successful, know that it is possible for you, too. Just because your friends win, doesn't mean you lose. There is enough wealth and success to go around here. Success is not a finite commodity. Believe in the sureness of your own success, and know that when the time is right, it will come together. Keep going.

WHAT HAPPENS WHEN YOUR ENEMIES BECOME SUCCESFUL

Rather than "Enemies", let's call this "Peers For Whom You Don't Much Care", or "PFWYDMC" for short. If you are in the same profession as your PFWYDMC, and they suddenly become successful while you continue to slave away unnoticed, it can create an insane amount of frustration and discontent in your life. Further exacerbating this discontent is the notion that you are better at your job than the PFWYDMC. "That dirty little PFWIDMC! I am SO much better than s/he is! Who did they f@ck to get that job?!" Honestly, we have all said it at one point or another.

Let me tell you something kids: your PFWYDMC may end up being just the flavor of the month, a flash in the pan, or, they may be really good. You may have to choke back the bile when they are accepting awards. Real success, real respect, comes from a continued demonstration of brilliance, and consistent, extraordinary performance on the job. If you are truly better than your PFWYDMC, continue to kick all kinds of ass in whatever you do. Cream rises to the top, but some sharks do, too. You will have to learn to swim with them without getting hurt. You should aim for longevity, and a good, solid body of work that clearly demonstrates outstanding achievement in your career.

WHAT IF IT HAPPENS TO YOUR BOYFRIEND/ GIRLFRIEND?

When large-scale success happens to the person closest to you in life—be it your boyfriend, girlfriend, spouse or partner—hang on to your hat! If you are in the same profession, it can be both exhilarating and inspiring to witness. There is no space for jealousy in this situation. If you find the green-eyed monster creeping over your shoulder, squash him immediately. Professional jealousy in a personal relationship signals the end. Your partner will need all the support you can give. You will see their sphere of influence change, you will witness the wave of new demands upon them, and you will observe a shift in the way he or she is regarded, in public and in private. You, as their partner, will need to be their touchstone of reality—the one solid thing in their life, when the rest of the world regards them as a commodity. You may benefit from their success as well, meeting new people and expanding your horizons. Be supportive of your partner, and look to their success to inspire your own.

LEARN FROM YOUR FRIENDS' EXPERIENCE

When your friends start to break through and become successful, watch carefully and learn from their experience. Observe their professional interactions, and determine if their dealings would be something you would choose to duplicate. If they handle a situation poorly, tuck it away in your brain so that you don't repeat it. Experience breakthrough success vicariously through your friends, and learn from their example. When it happens to you, you will have a leg up on how to conduct yourself.

WHAT IF IT HAPPENS TO YOU?

What if *you* are the first of your friends to break through? How do you deal with the pressure and responsibility of leading the pack? How do you maintain a graceful existence with your friends and family, knowing that they may have feelings of jealousy and resentment toward you because of it?

Keep your center, and keep your success in perspective. Remember that, while you may have achieved something meaningful in your field, you are not the President of the United States, you are not Mahatma Ghandi, and you are not saving Tibet or curing cancer! In the big picture of life, you work in the entertainment industry, helping to create art that enables people to forget about life for a while. Do not adopt a sense of entitlement, or superiority to your friends and family. Do not brag about your accomplishments; let your family do the kvelling for you. Stay humble, and realize that you have a lot of work ahead of you to ensure real, sustained success in your career. You will have to continue to do excellent work, raising the bar not for everyone else, but for yourself as well.

INTERVIEW

Subject: Mike Dougherty
Writer
Credits include: *X2*, *X-Men 3*

Hometown: Columbus, OH
Moved to LA: 2000

Topic: Keeping Centered in the Whirlwind of Success

Where did you go to school/what did you study?

I went to NYU Tisch School of the Arts, where I studied film and television with a heavy emphasis on sick and twisted animation.

How did you decide to come to Los Angeles?

After living in New York for eight years, the siren call of Los Angeles became too hard to resist. New York is a great place to live and get your feet wet, and I think everyone should do it at some point, but if you want to do film, LA is really where you need to be.

Did you have any contacts here (personal or business) and how did they help you in setting yourself up here?

I was lucky enough to have a good circle of friends already living in LA who were working in the industry, and that was immensely helpful both personally and professionally. They provided couches to crash on while apartment hunting, they would lend advice on how to get started, and also became close collaborators that I still work with today.

How did you find your writing partner?

We met at the last performance of "CATS" in New York. I'm not kidding. Neither of us are musical theater buffs, but a mutual friend had tickets so we both ended up going. It was surreal. We kind of lost touch after that, but one day I found out he moved to LA and was living in a house just around the corner. After that we started hanging out a lot more often and decided to unite our evil powers.

How did you get an agent?

When I was still living in New York, the William Morris Agency started to dabble in the emerging internet content boom and created a "New Media" division. Since I had a pretty strong background in animation and internet technology, they started representing me in that arena. Later, the internet boom went bust, and as I started migrating toward screenwriting and moved to LA, the New York agents referred me to their colleagues on the west coast. I quickly learned that even though I was repped by the New Media division, it wasn't going to be easy to get a lit agent. They still wanted to see a spec script or other material, and that became another motivating factor to sit down and start writing.

When did you realize that you were successful?

Honestly, I don't know if I've ever had that realization, or if I ever want to. That might sound like false humility, but it's true, and I also think it's a healthy insecurity to have in order to keep yourself grounded and motivated. I always want to feel like I have something to prove, and I'm afraid that if I start believing I'm "successful" that I might lose some of that drive. Also, there's nothing worse than writer who thinks their own shit doesn't stink.

How do you keep your center in this competitive business?

Friends. I can't emphasize that enough. You need a healthy balance of friends/collaborators who you can trust and work with, but you also need to keep the friends you had before you jumped into the snake pit. Friends who work in the industry are great because they can lend advice and understand the difficulties of the business, while friends on the outside are often the ones who aren't afraid to give you their honest opinions…something that is rare in this town.

How do you "keep the love alive" in your writing partnership (when there are jealousies or conflicts of opinion)?

Besides being writing partners, Dan and I are great friends, so we're not afraid to butt heads and call each other assholes when necessary. When we were on X-MEN 2, fighting over ideas was just a part of the daily grind, and if Bryan Singer taught us anything, it's that healthy debate usually only leads to better ideas. Dan and I also developed this strange writing method where we're constantly emailing our scripts back and forth to rewrite each other, and we never take it personally when one changes the other's work. Plus, at the end of the day we'll usually close the laptops, order a pizza and vegetate with some insane cartoons and trashy reality television.

What kinds of responsibilities or duties (to others) compel you now due to your success?

I don't know if I'd call it a sense of responsibility or duty, but there is part of me that wants to make the type of movies that inspired me when I was younger. I'd love nothing more than to know that in twenty or thirty years, some other kid in Ohio is watching something I worked on, and gets the crazy idea in his head that he should pick up a camcorder and start making movies too.

How has success/fame altered your relationships (friends, family, people at home)?

I think it's strengthened a lot of my personal relationships. I find that as you get older and more entrenched in the industry, you start to realize what's really important is the people you surround yourself with. Friends and family become more valuable than ever, because they're the ones that you can turn to when the professional side of your life becomes too overwhelming.

Any reflections about the path you've chosen that you would like to share?

Do what you love. Yeah I know, it sounds like cheap fortune cookie wisdom, but it's true. If you want to be a screenwriter, then write a movie YOU would want to see on the screen. Don't try to write something just for the sake of selling it or because you think it's what's "hot". I'm a huge horror fan, so my first spec script was the type of old-school horror film that I've always wanted to see on the big screen. Even though the horror genre was pretty much dead back then, I didn't try to write a romantic comedy or sports movie. I don't love those kinds of films, so if I attempted to write one it would probably come across as forced and passionless. Write what you know, and write what you love.

CHAPTER TEN

REAL SUCCESS/FAME/MONEY

The ultimate goal for many people in the entertainment industry is real, earned success, accompanied by fame and money. It is actually an attainable goal, and if you persevere, you can get there. You will find, once you do, that there are good things and bad things to say about success, fame and money. You will have a host of new concerns: employees, businesses, homes in four cities. You may even build an empire for yourself, branching into different areas of the entertainment business. It will change your life.

REALITY CHECK

There are good parts and bad parts to achieving success/fame/money. The good parts include: professional recognition, expanded influence in society, bigger projects, more money, broader professional options, and fame. You may develop a fan base, and have the opportunity to travel the world promoting your work. You may be able to translate your professional success into a charitable cause, or a pet project, using your influence to secure funding or publicity. You will undoubtedly have a sense of accomplishment and feel like you have found your place in the world.

The downside of success/fame/money is that the world knows who you are and what you have. You may be constantly asked for money or charitable contributions, by outsiders and by friends and family. You may make more money than anyone in your family, and they may resent you for it. Your family may have expectations of you supporting them financially, whether you intend to or not. You may attract stalkers or paparazzi, or the delightful combo—*stalkerazzi*. You may cultivate a reputation, good or bad, that may be difficult to change once it has been established. You may live your life in public—every mistake or defeat in your world becomes a matter for public discussion. You may become restless, having met all of your goals.

MAKING NEW GOALS

It is time to revisit the STOP-START-CONTINUE list, and make adjustments where necessary. Take your time and plot your next move carefully. Achieving wide-scale success is part of the "rebirth" process. You are now free to use your powerful influence to chart your own course.

You may find yourself in charge of large departments within an organization, whether it is a studio, agency, or production team. You may start thinking about establishing your own production company, developing your own projects from the ground up. Suddenly, you become more than just yourself, and the work with your name on it becomes a team effort. You will likely feel profound responsibility, not just for your own work duties, but also for the livelihoods of others. People will depend on you for their job, their paycheck, and their health insurance. You will have employees under your leadership, and you will have all of the headaches and all of the joys that accompany these responsibilities.

You will also need to be concerned with the quality of work coming out with your name on it. One of the most important tasks in front of you is to stock your office team with the best workforce you can find. Once the resumes start to pour in, where do you begin?

WHO'S THE BOSS?

Hiring a competent workforce is crucial to your continued success. Your employees are going to be the ones who represent you in public, and whom you hold accountable for the way your work is done. What should you look for? The answer is simple: the best people, period.

1) <u>Specific Answers to Specific Questions</u>
   When you interview a potential candidate, ask specific questions. If they give you concise, specific answers, they are likely telling the truth. Concise answers point to the candidate's attention to detail, something that is crucial in this business.

   Example: I see you worked on <u>Great Big Movie X</u>. What was your involvement in the project?
   Good answer: "I was the Assistant Production Coordinator in Los Angeles for three months."
   Bad answer: "I kinda helped out for a while, answered phones, did runs, you know."

Your future employees will be answering questions pertaining to *your* business—wouldn't you prefer they have concise, specific answers to the questions they will be asked about you and your projects? Attention to detail is very important, and concise communication is a very basic indicator of their skill level in this area.

2) Work Ethic
Check their background. Call their references. Ask the candidate to tell you what they enjoyed about their last job. If you perceive that they have a sense of joy about what they do, their work ethic will likely be strong. Finally, check their fingernails. If you work in production, where hours are long and the work is not only intellectually intense, but physical, check their fingernails. Beautiful, fussily manicured nails have no place in the production world. You need someone who will pitch in, get their hands dirty, and work until the task is finished.

3) Self-Motivated
Hiring individuals who are self-motivated will save you time and headache. You will not have to micro-manage someone who is a self-starter. They will manage themselves. When you check their references, be sure to ask about their level of self-motivation, and their sense of pride about their work. When you find someone who is a true self-starter, with a sense of pride in a job well-done, snag them.

4) Discipline
The combination of discipline with self-motivation creates a powerhouse of an employee. With employees like this, you will be able to kick more ass as a team than you could ever imagine. Ask their former employers about their sense of focus, and their ability to stick to the task at hand. The candidate doesn't have to be a boring, workaholic fart to be disciplined—just make sure that the candidate displays the qualities associated with disciplined action: consistency, thoroughness, follow-through, attention to detail, quality care, and respect.

5) Superheroes in the Hall of Justice
When assembling your team, think of them as Superheroes in the Hall of Justice. Every Superhero has their one special power, their secret weapon, that makes them invincible. So, too, should your employees possess a super-power. Fill your office, or your department with people like *Brainiac*, *SuperEgoSmoother*, *ProblemBuster*, and *The Persuader*.

> Encourage your employees to develop their super-powers and hone them to a sharp point. Working together, the Superheroes never lose.

Do not give in to the temptation to just "hire bodies". Hiring any-old-anyone just because you need people will not do you any good in the long run. Choose your employees, even day players, with care. Build an effective team.

Another temptation you might want to resist is hiring your friends and family. While it is wonderful to have a work environment filled with friends, it is risky to hire them *INTO* a work environment. You may find that your position of authority makes it difficult to manage your friends or family or to even offer up constructive criticism. Sometimes there is a shocking display of undisciplined behavior because the employee/friend feels "too comfortable" and has a sense of job security whether or not they perform well. It is extremely difficult to be in a position where you are forced to fire your friend or family member. Consider your options carefully when hiring.

Before you hire your new employees, be sure to check their references carefully. Ask their former employers about the candidate's strengths and weaknesses, and the circumstances under which they parted company. If you really like the candidate, make sure that you have not been *blinded by the light*—one great trait in the candidate has overshadowed the bad traits. Be measured and judicious in your assessment of the candidate. Before you make an offer, carefully discuss the salary and perks of the position with your accountant, so that everyone is clear and up-front about what the offer entails.

STRIKING UP THE BAND

Once you have hired the best people you can find, let them shine.

1) <u>Treat Employees with Respect</u>
   Acknowledge that you chose them because you believe in them. Do not give the employee bullshit praise to encourage them. With the right employees on your team, they will not need praise as encouragement, and they will see through your insincere attempts. Your employees will know when they have done a job well. Give them praise when it is deserved, and mean it.

2) <u>Encourage "Team Spirit"</u>
   Before you start to work together, gather all the employees for dinner, drinks, game night, bowling, you name it. Allow your employees to

bond on a social level before they begin to work together. People will work together more effectively when they feel comfortable with one another. You can go so far as to buy and distribute team t-shirts, tiaras, magic wands—it will galvanize your employees. Do what you can to make every employee feel valuable as a team member.

3) Set A Good Example
You are not just the boss, you are the one who sets the tone. What you expect of your employees, expect of yourself. If there is work to be done that you would not ordinarily do, but your employees are overloaded, get off your butt and help them. Your employees will gain more respect for you for the fact that you will be there for them whenever they need you. Be sure to conduct yourself professionally and diplomatically in your business dealings. Your employees are paying attention, believe it or not. The quickest way to engender loyalty and respect in your employees is to demonstrate that you are the kind of boss they are proud to represent.

4) Remember That There Is A Person In There
Your team is not comprised of robots, and as an employer, you need to be sensitive to the person inside the employee. We all have good days and bad days, and even under the most extraordinary pressure, you must remember that work is just *work*. Your employees have lives beyond your business. While there may be "crunch" times that require overtime, do not make your employees continually sacrifice their personal lives for the sake of work. When appropriate, encourage lunch-time visits from their spouses or family. Continue to gather employees and their families for parties, game nights, and barbeques. Recognize and respect your employees' personal space and need for a life outside of work.

5) Do Not Micro-Manage
In order to completely circumvent the need to micro-manage, you must hire self-motivated people for your team. You can check in with your employees, and touch base with them, but ultimately you must *trust* them. Hire the right people in the first place, and let them kick some ass. If you do not hire the right people, you will be micro-managing until the end of time, and you will lose faith in their ability to do their job. Micro-managing is exhausting, and it turns out to be more

work than it is worth. Hire the right people from the get-go, and relieve yourself of this offensive duty.

6) Do Not Overlook Job Performance Problems
You may run into situations where an employee has a job performance problem. For example, s/he may have made a huge clerical error on an important contract that gets sent to the head of Great Big Studio X. There is nothing you can do about the fact that a mistake was made this time, but it behooves you to talk with your employee immediately to ensure that it never happens again. If the employee continues to let things slip through the cracks, you will need to let the person go. Do not let your employees become a liability to you and your work. Move immediately to address performance problems with your employees. If you fail to do so, your entire team could suffer as a result. You could see low morale, and sloppy work in otherwise good employees. If they think the boss doesn't care, then why should they? In ignoring performance problems, you risk alienating your employees, and giving them an unfavorable impression of you, their boss.

Being the boss is not easy, but you can make it a lot easier on yourself by getting the right employees on your team. Encourage them to develop their skills and lead them to be the best they can be. If, after their stint of work with you, they go on to be successful leaders in their own right, you have done your job well.

NA-NA-NA-NA…HEY-HEY-HEY

It is inevitable that you will, at some point, have to fire someone. This is one of the hardest things to do as an employer. It doesn't really matter how you do it—you can be nice, understanding, and sweet; you can be cold, aloof, and antiseptic—the person is going to go to bed that night without a job. Do your best to avoid a harsh outburst or reprimand, even if the employee has really messed up. Further, do not fire your employee in public, making a mockery of him/her. Allow your employee the dignity to receive this news in private, so they can collect their thoughts in peace. When the employee has left the building, do not trash him/her when talking with your other employees. Certainly the fired employee had buddies at work, and they will definitely hear about it if you speak ill of them after they leave. Be respectful of the person inside the employee, even if they behaved like a nincompoop on the job.

WRAPPING UP A JOB

When your employee's term of employment ends, there are some things you can do to provide for much-needed closure.

1) Exit Polling

   You may want to provide your employees with a feedback forum. This can help you as an employer to know how effective you have been, and how to improve your leadership skills. These polls can be tremendously helpful to employees as well. You can provide employees with a written evaluation from you to them, and they can fill out an evaluation for you, rating your performance. Filling out evaluations in writing is faster and more concise than a lengthy exit interview, but make sure that you schedule time with your employees to discuss the evaluations to answer any questions they might have.

   The following are two examples of exit polls, both from employer to employee, and from employee to employer. While these are good guideline documents, use your own sensibilities to design questions and comments suitable to your needs.

<< Sample Exit Poll from employee to boss >>

EMPLOYEE NAME:______________________________________

Circle Answers

How would you rate your job satisfaction in the following areas (1 is low, 10 is high):

I felt like I made a significant impact at work:
① ② ③ ③ ④ ⑤ ⑥ ⑦ ⑧ ⑨ ⑩

I felt like my voice was heard by my supervisors:
① ② ③ ③ ④ ⑤ ⑥ ⑦ ⑧ ⑨ ⑩

I felt like part of a team:
① ② ③ ③ ④ ⑤ ⑥ ⑦ ⑧ ⑨ ⑩

I had enough time and adequate supplies to do my work:
① ② ③ ③ ④ ⑤ ⑥ ⑦ ⑧ ⑨ ⑩

I was given clear instruction and direction to perform my work:
① ② ③ ③ ④ ⑤ ⑥ ⑦ ⑧ ⑨ ⑩

I learned something new, improved my skills:
① ② ③ ③ ④ ⑤ ⑥ ⑦ ⑧ ⑨ ⑩

I felt proud of my work:
① ② ③ ③ ④ ⑤ ⑥ ⑦ ⑧ ⑨ ⑩

I felt appreciated:
① ② ③ ③ ④ ⑤ ⑥ ⑦ ⑧ ⑨ ⑩

I would work with this team again:
① ② ③ ③ ④ ⑤ ⑥ ⑦ ⑧ ⑨ ⑩

Any additional comments:

____

____

____

<< Sample Exit Poll from Boss to employee >>

EMPLOYEE NAME:____

Circle Answers

Rate employee's performance in the following areas (1—low, 10—high):

Takes direction:
① ② ③ ③ ④ ⑤ ⑥ ⑦ ⑧ ⑨ ⑩

Thoroughly completes assignments:
① ② ③ ③ ④ ⑤ ⑥ ⑦ ⑧ ⑨ ⑩

Displays technical knowledge of work process:
① ② ③ ③ ④ ⑤ ⑥ ⑦ ⑧ ⑨ ⑩

Works well independently; self-disciplined:
① ② ③ ③ ④ ⑤ ⑥ ⑦ ⑧ ⑨ ⑩

Concentration/focus on job at hand:
① ② ③ ③ ④ ⑤ ⑥ ⑦ ⑧ ⑨ ⑩

Attention to detail:
① ② ③ ③ ④ ⑤ ⑥ ⑦ ⑧ ⑨ ⑩

Follow-through:
① ② ③ ③ ④ ⑤ ⑥ ⑦ ⑧ ⑨ ⑩

Brings forth innovative and creative solutions to problems:
① ② ③ ③ ④ ⑤ ⑥ ⑦ ⑧ ⑨ ⑩

Overall work ethic:
① ② ③ ③ ④ ⑤ ⑥ ⑦ ⑧ ⑨ ⑩

Is diplomatic and cooperative with co-workers:
① ② ③ ③ ④ ⑤ ⑥ ⑦ ⑧ ⑨ ⑩

Is diplomatic and cooperative with supervisors:
① ② ③ ③ ④ ⑤ ⑥ ⑦ ⑧ ⑨ ⑩

Additional comments:____

2) Thank You Gifts and Cards
   The acknowledgement of a job well done is one of the most fun duties of an employer. When your job is over, or when your employee leaves your company to pursue other opportunities, make sure they know how much you have appreciated their time and effort on your behalf. You don't need to provide them with an expensive Caribbean Cruise Package or brand-new car; in fact, leave the notion of expensive gifts behind. Rather, put some thought into a thank-you gift that suits their personality. A thoughtful gift, something that is meaningful to the recipient, doesn't have to be expensive. Get creative. If you have a large team, don't go broke on the thank-you gifts. A personal, eloquent, hand-written card goes a long way toward expressing your gratitude. No matter what form of expression you choose, just do it. Your employees will really appreciate it.

3) Letters of Recommendation
   Another way to say thank you to your employees is to write them a letter of recommendation without their having to ask. Upon completion of a job, present your employee with a signed letter of recommendation detailing their magnificent performance and stellar skills. Avail yourself for referrals and *mean it.* Do not give a letter of recommendation to an employee who has not handily earned it. Your words, in the form of a letter of recommendation, can really make a difference to the employee's self-esteem. This unsolicited gesture of support will leave them with a lasting impression of your appreciation for them.

I'M CALLING ON A REFERENCE FOR…

You may receive phone calls from potential employers looking to hire one of your former employees. Some companies have strict policies in place regarding employment verification, due to fear of legal action. Usually these policies dictate that you, as the former employer, can only say, "Person X worked here from (date) to (date) and earned $X." Check with your boss or your HR department if you work at a larger company that may have instituted a similar plan.

If you are a freelance employer, or if you own your own company, it is a different story. When asked to give a reference, and the employee was or is a good one, this is a no-brainer. Download the love-fest to the potential employer. Gush, freestyle, in fifty colors. But what do you say when you have concerns or misgivings about the employee? If your impressions are 75% positive or higher, speak kindly (and honestly) about the employee. If your impressions are 74% positive or lower, keep your mouth shut. Literally, keep your mouth shut. People here in Los Angeles are savvy enough to know what that means; you don't have to explain yourself. You don't have to return the potential employer's call, either. One way to avoid having to speak negatively about a candidate is to not take the phone call.

Why avoid saying negative things? Call it karma, or superstition, what goes around comes around. You don't <u>need</u> to say negative things about a job candidate, even if they were a complete imbecile. Deliberately saying *nothing* is more effective than potentially opening a can of worms in saying something negative. And who needs the reputation for trashing former employees? Navigate this part of the business with aplomb. Be clear in your appraisal of the employee. Whether you say, "The candidate is a must hire! Superb!" or "I have nothing to say; read my lips:————————", make sure that the potential employer understands your recommendation.

INTERVIEW

Subject: Holly Wiersma
Producer
Credits Include: *Wonderland, Happy Endings, Down in the Valley*

Hometown: Amherst, OH
Moved to LA: 1996

Topic: Building an Empire

How did you decide on a career in the entertainment industry?

I always knew I wanted to be in the entertainment industry. My uncle was on *Saturday Night Live* when I was very young. He played the character "Father Guido Sarducci." He was also a writer on the show for many years so I would go and visit him in NY and that is how I got a "touch" of this business.

How did you ascend to the title of Producer?

I started out as a casting director. My uncle's girlfriend at the time, Davia Nelson, did casting/producing for Zoetrope (Francis Ford Coppola's company). She was helping cast *The Rainmaker,* which Francis was directing, and invited me to come up to Northern California and intern in the extras casting department.

When I was up there, I met the Extras Casting Director who lived in LA and promised me a job answering phones and filing in Los Angeles on a couple of his new films. I was so excited that I was going to be in the movie business. I called everyone at home and told them.

On my first day, I arrived at his home/office to find out from his assistant (who was handing me the keys and quitting because she had not been paid in a month) that he had gone out of town. I ended up going into the office, and I just started answering the phones and learning (from the hundreds of extras coming by and calling) what to do. Of course, they were very excited because I was helping them get their SAG cards.

When he returned, he gave me my very own movie to do (casting/hiring of extras), which was *Blade.* I spent a lot of time on that set learning what people's jobs were and I actually became friends with some of the actors...two of them being Stephen Dorff and Donal Logue, who informed me that I should be making more than $300.00 a week, but I didn't care because I was making movies.

After that I got a call from Fred Roos' (casting director/producer of *The Godfather, The Outsiders,* etc...) office, who offered me a chance to intern with him, which I did, and I started to get into principal casting, which is something that I thought I really wanted to do. I then started getting projects that people were asking me to cast...the catch was that none of these projects were financed.

One day I got a call from a producer who said that he had a project with the financing but with no actors attached. Through my contacts I was able to help them get Balthazar Getty, for which, in return, I received an associate producer credit and $2,500.00. That was the first time that I really started thinking about producing. My second script (a friend of a friend sent to me) was called *Comic*

Book Villains. This is when I went to my friend Donal Logue and asked him to be in the movie. Lions Gate ended up making this movie for under two million dollars in the year 2000.

Have you set up a production company/incorporated?

Yes, I have set up a small production company that has been incorporated. It is just me and I have two assistants.

At what point in your career did you decide to do this & why did you feel that it was the right time, or advantageous, to do so?

It just sort of happened. I started getting great scripts that, as a viewer, I wanted to go and see.

How long did it take to get things up and running?

It has taken me about 4 years.

What is the employee hiring process like (in the office as well as on a film)?

I think that you have to look for people that are passionate, talented, and will work well with other people. As far as on the set—I think you look for people that are still excited about the prospect of making movies and for whom it has not become just a job.

What qualities do you look for in potential employees & what shortcomings, if any, can you overlook?

I look for people that are driven, passionate, reliable, and trustworthy. It is fine if people don't have loads of experience as long as they are willing to learn.

Did anyone give you good guidance or advice along the way to becoming a movie mogul & what was it?

I was always advised never to spend your own money on your projects, but I have never listened.

How many projects have you (and/or your company) produced?

I have produced 6 movies-
Shadow Hours
Rent Control

Comic Book Villains
Wonderland
Down In The Valley
Happy Endings
Dot (in pre-production)

Any surprises along the way?

I think every movie is surprise! Every day, each movie is starting over. There are problems and things you didn't even think about on the last one…

CHAPTER ELEVEN

KEEPING IT REAL & PASSING IT ON

So you're on your way to becoming a Tinseltown mogul. How do you *not* become a cheesy Hollywood sleaze-ball? What turns a person into a sleaze? Some folks are just plain lazy, and they slip into sleazy behavior because everyone else is doing it. Nobody really likes it, but sleaze continues to exist. Instead of fighting (sleaze) fire with (sleaze) fire, how about fighting (sleaze) fire with (integrity) water? You are in for a battle, but you will appreciate the strength and purpose your integrity gives you when faced with some of Hollywood's more notorious offenses, and so will your cohorts.

Behavior is a choice, no matter how you feel. If you are frustrated or angry, it is your choice whether to a) bludgeon someone's car with a golf club, b) scream bloody murder at your assistant, or c) take out your aggression at the batting cages. Bad behavior will come back to you in the form of escalating sleaze-whiff. Before you know it, you will begin to reek of sleaze, and pretty soon there will be no turning back. Look carefully at your behavioral choices to avoid becoming a sleaze-ball.

Clearly, there is a difference between sleaze-whiff (which gets on you when you brush up against or participate in sleazy activity) and being a sleaze-ball (immersion in sleaze culture to the degree that it is second-nature). There is a difference between having a few dings on your record, and living a life of sleaze. That fact notwithstanding, if you wake up one morning and realize that you have become a fully soaked sleaze-ball, do not despair; you do not have to stay that way. The good news is that there is always redemption for sleaze-balls, but you have to really want to change your life.

CHOICES

No one forces you to be a sleaze. In the Hollywood environment, you can dig your own sleazy grave with bad behavioral choices. The following are some situations that could potentially plunge you into the sleaze-ifier:

1) Big Bad Ego

   We have all heard legends of Hollywood's most notorious egomaniacs. These are the people who have heard, listened to, and believed all of the hype ever printed about them. They are masters of their own universe, and we are just extras in the grand picture of their life. Other ways to describe the Big Bad Ego: arrogance, bitchiness, pomposity, superiority, pretentiousness, entitlement, imperiousness, snootiness. These are the people who condescend, patronize, and throw disparaging remarks like javelins. They may have millions of dollars in the bank from their box office hits, but they are shockingly destitute in their soul.

   Some suggestions to prevent this: Cultivate compassion. Volunteer your time, not your money, with the less-fortunate. Spend some time getting to know your inner self. Seek to understand people who are different from you, and develop compassion for all people.

2) Rage And Violence

   An astonishing number of people in Hollywood have anger management problems so severe that, if channeled, could provide enough raw electricity to solve California's energy crisis. Rage is a crippling affliction that not only consumes its host, but affects everyone around him/her. Violence, the end-result of rage, is a consequence no rational person would wish on anyone. Rage can be manifested in everything from silent seething to screaming tirades, throwing of objects, destruction of property, and physical beatings. Some offenders take particular glee in scaring the bejeezus out of their employees and associates with their tirades. You may not even be able to recognize that you have an anger management problem. If you walk through the office and people cower in fear, take that as a hint. Screaming at your employees is not normal or professional behavior. Throwing objects at them, or at the wall, is not normal behavior. In fact, it is attempted assault. Uncontrolled rage is not just a sleaze-ifier, it is potentially a trip to jail.

Some suggestions to prevent this: Go directly into therapy. Your rage triggers may stem from incidents in childhood you can no longer identify, and it will take the work of a gifted therapist to help you to unwrap the mystery of your rage. Physical activities like hitting golf balls, going to the batting cages, and chopping wood may be good short-term solutions, but they will not solve the problem. You must do the work!

3) Drug Use
If you want to do X at Burning Man, fine. If you want to smoke weed and do somersaults in Griffith Park, have fun. However, the moment you do drugs in the work environment, you are in trouble. If you find yourself at an office party at your boss' house snorting a line of coke off of a naked 19-year-old's body, you are a complete sleaze. Recreational intoxicants have no place in the work environment, and that also means at work-sponsored events. Overuse or abuse of recreational intoxicants, even outside of work, will give you sleaze-whiff. Snorting an eight-ball and driving to Mexico for a five-day bender will definitely leave you stinking of sleaze. Dealing drugs, even casually to friends, will drench you in sleaze-whiff. Further, if you drive while hopped up on intoxicants, are caught possessing them, or dealing them, it can land you in jail.

Some suggestions to prevent this: The quick solution is to not do drugs period; they are illegal. However, let's get real. If you must imbibe, keep your use of recreational intoxicants to a minimum, occasional level. Do not brag about your drug-addled exploits, or the excellent quality of chronic you pimped from your friends in Cypress Hill. If you have a drug problem, a physical or psychological addiction to a drug, seek treatment in a rehabilitation facility or through Narcotics Anonymous.

4) Duplicity, Lying, Double-Dealing: Greed
As adults, we are supposed to know the difference between right and wrong. Why then, do some people insist on doing the double-cross? Stress changes behavior, especially if the individual is not prepared for it. You will observe outright lies, people working both ends of a deal, telling clients what they want to hear instead of the truth. This behavior is often tied to greed—whether for money, power, or sex—or all of them at once. The lines between reality and fabrication become

blurred in the servitude of greed. You may witness co-workers dropping lies to cover their asses or to inflate their own importance. Liars and bullshitters are easily sniffed out here, even the good ones. Sleaze reek smells an awful lot like bullshit.

Some suggestions to prevent this: Hold yourself accountable for the truth. There is no other way to avoid lying but to NOT LIE. You choose your behavior, and you can put an end to duplicity in your life. If you have a real, deep-seated problem, consult a mental health professional to get at the root of why you feel compelled to lie. Your life will improve dramatically if you can get the help you need to solve your problem.

5) <u>Porn, Soft-Core, or "Adult Entertainment"</u>

Yes that's correct: even soft-core. Some people think that working for Playboy doesn't count as working in Porn. You talk with the people at Playboy. They will refer to their business as "adult entertainment", which is just a nice way of saying Porn. The fact remains that "adult entertainment" is a different business from the mainstream, legit entertainment industry. There are many among us here who have worked for Playboy. Let's be clear: nudity is not the enemy. *Sexualized* nudity causes the sleaze-whiff. "Adult entertainment" is a different planet than Hollywood. People who work in "adult entertainment" often come to the table with their own personal baggage about sexuality. Watching two people simulate, or heck, actually perform sex for ten hours a day can desensitize even the most healthy, grounded person. If it is your dream to work in the "adult entertainment" industry, you will never find a shortage of employment. However, realize that a resume filled with porn titles will get you nowhere when you want to advance your career.

Some suggestions to prevent this: Do not participate in the production of porn, soft-core or "adult entertainment". Say no to these job offers, even if you are flat broke. There is nothing wrong with temping.

6) <u>Criminal Behavior</u>

Criminal behavior in this film industry includes, but is not limited to: fraud, copyright infringement, embezzlement, plagiarism, property theft (intellectual or physical), rescinding offers of employment, and breach of contract. These issues are complicated, because they involve a chain of events that leads to the commission of a crime. Perhaps you didn't set out to defraud your investors of $15 million, but gee it sure turned out that way when you have nothing to show for it two years later. You may align yourself with a business partner who drags you into the sleaze-pit because of his or her dirty dealings. Engaging in criminal behavior is the end-all-be-all of sleaze. It can also land you in jail or prison.

Some suggestions to prevent this: Look before you leap into business deals. If someone feels shady, or reeks of sleaze-whiff, do not go into business with them. If you find that your partner has perpetrated some illegal dirty dealings, get some legal help immediately.

7) Using Sex As A Weapon, Tool, or Reward
There are plenty of perpetrators of this bad behavior choice. The promise of sexual fulfillment is an alluring carrot at the end of the stick. There are plenty of weak people in Hollywood who fall for this trick every time. You will likely face this scenario at least once in your career: someone wants something from you, they shimmy up to you and wink, nudge, nudge. Do you take the bait? Only if you want to get played. Sniff around for the trace of something rank. Do not trust anyone who offers you the promise of sex for professional favors. Further, do not expect to be taken seriously if you perpetrate the use of sex for favors. Contrary to the myth of the casting couch, sleeping with a director will NOT guarantee you a job on his/her next movie. In fact, such an act can engender serious disrespect for you and your career objectives. If you force the issue, using your sexual knowledge of the person as a weapon, you will reek of sleaze, and you will lose your self-respect in the process.

Some suggestions to prevent this: Don't fling your kitty around looking for favors; don't wink and nudge, expecting people to reward you with jobs, money, benefits. Just don't do it. It's manipulative and sincerely sleazy.

No matter what is going on in your life, no matter how sad or empty or frustrated you feel, your behavior is a choice. No one forces you to be a sleaze. Your behavioral choices will speak for themselves; choose wisely and be strong. Keep it real.

HOLDING YOUR GROUND

Living your life and pursuing your Hollywood career with integrity can sometimes feel like a tall order. There are so many obstacles to overcome, and so many crossroads at which you could choose a sleazy path or a path of integrity. Stick to your guns. Set a better example and raise the bar. Command respect. If you earn the reputation of being a straight shooter, the other straight shooters in Hollywood are going to want to do business with you. Cultivate this reputation, and seek out people who share your perspective on the business. Pass on a better role model to those who come after you. Build a better legacy for this business than the one that existed when you arrived here.

PASSING IT ON & GIVING BACK

When you get to a position in your career where you can help people, knock yourself out. Be generous with your help; don't be stingy for fear of "competition". Chances are, anyone you are powerful enough to help will not be your competition. Share your knowledge of projects or positions that might appeal to a young upstart you know. Confident people do not fear competition; they encourage it. Aim for a legacy of people who are better in their field because of your influence. Do not withhold information to thwart the development of any person in this business. Think strategically; hook people up with each other when you see a link that could be beneficial to both parties.

You can also give back by teaching. Take on interns and show them the ropes. Accept the responsibility of grooming the next crop of Hollywood heavies. Teach, lecture, or volunteer at schools, colleges and universities. Share your knowledge with those who are interested in your field. This business is small, and your knowledge will be specific. There are not many people in the world who do exactly what you do; educate and enlighten those who would like to pursue a career in your field. Encourage and develop raw talent when you see it. Be gracious when former students thank you for your time and support. Encourage them to do the same for others.

INTERVIEW

Subject: Tony Okungbowa
TV Personality
Credits include: ***The Ellen Degeneres Show***

Hometown: London, UK
Moved to LA: 1998

Topic: Keeping it Real

How did you come to Los Angeles?

I used to work for a company called Diesel, a fashion company that moved me here because they needed a position filled. I used to be their West Coast sales representative for men's clothing and accessories. They also knew that I was in the entertainment industry and I was going to need to make that transition sooner or later, so they were kind enough to marry sort of both of them together, and they helped me move out here from New York.

How do you feel about being here in Hollywood?

Hollywood, actually, has been good to me. It really, truly has. It's one of those places where you can find a lot of what you want if you look for it. It's kind of, in a way, like New York, but New York is different because it's at your fingertips and there's more of a vibrancy to New York. Hollywood is that place where you can go and shut your door and not have to go out and socialize if you choose to…or you can go and socialize if you choose to…so, it's been good to me; it's also brought me a lot more financial stability and a lot more exposure and I guess celebrity, if you want to call it that. It's been good to me on the whole.

Does Los Angeles feel like "home"?

Partly, yes. I mean, based on the fact that I actually *own* a home here, so…it's the first place I've actually bought a house, so to a certain degree it does feel like a home. Given the choice of a place to call my home, with money and work not being a factor, it wouldn't be my home. But as it stands right now, it is—and you know, it's quite a comfortable one at that. Yeah; it is home for now.

How do you describe the "sleaze factor" here; how pervasive is it?

I feel it exists in every city. The fact that this place is the media capital of the world, so to speak, makes it a bit more obvious, I guess, or a bit more in your face—but it does exist in every major city in the world, because I've been blessed to live in those places.

I was talking to a pretty well-known actor the other day and I was asking him, "How do you deal with everything—" His response was: "If you let it get to you, it gets to you." If you let the sleaze attach itself to you, then there comes a lot of drama with it. I just brush it off and just think, "I feel sorry for you (those who perpetrate the 'sleaze factor') that you have to do that," or if the sleaze comes around me, I try to extricate myself from it.

How do you deal with the sleaze factor in LA?

By surrounding myself with real people—people who know *me*. A great way to extricate yourself from it or to keep away from it is to involve yourself in other things, things outside the industry. Ironically, as a person in the industry, whether you're an actor or a writer or a musician, or a director—whatever it is, casting directors have told me that the more interesting actors or the people that they've met are people who have other interests besides acting. I have a friend who was a woman waiting out her younger years to have a baby because of her career. As soon as she had a baby, she started booking (jobs), because there were more interesting things going on in her life.

So I think that the more you involve yourself in things outside of the industry, which tend to have sleaze with them (the industry, that is) the more you are able to disassociate yourself from it, and things become water off a duck's back, when that thing comes around you, and that's one way I've been able to do that. I really just involve myself in other things that have more of a concrete base. It's almost like an anchor for me; I find things that will become an anchor for me outside of the industry.

How do you keep your center when Hollywood erupts with demands for your time?

A big part of it is my spirituality. I am really lucky that I am on a journey that affords me the opportunity to explore my spirituality. Also the fact that I have family in a place that is a developing nation, I hate to use the words "3rd-world country"; it's a developing country, and I call them up and they don't have all the glorious amenities that we have in this country, or in England for that fact, and they live in Nigeria and I have to send money home sometimes, and I have to make sure that they're okay, and they can't just get on a plane and come visit because they can't get visas, so that in itself, above everything else, is an extremely humbling experience. Every time I feel kind of shaky, I go to the rock. It's an old hymn, actually, *I Go to the Rock That Brings Salvation.* I actually *do* go to the rock, which is just to pick up the phone and call those guys. I mean, I send $1000 to them and it lasts for like four months. While I go to a store in Hollywood, because I've got to go to a premiere, or I've got to go to the Emmys and present there and the shirt costs $1000, and I'm like: "Okay!! Reality CHECK!" My family in Africa is a real anchoring factor for me. It's a humbling thing, and that keeps it real for me.

I'm in New York for the Emmys and walking down the red carpet and there're people screaming my name and there are cameras flashing, and I'm just thinking: "My dad, in his wildest dreams, would never get this, would never, ever get this." It's just a very surreal experience when you know what it's like with my brother. It's just really humbling, and it makes you keep it in perspective.

How much a part does your spirituality play in keeping your head straight?

For me, because my family is not here...you can really get caught up in this town. People will tell you everything they want you to hear, in order to get what they want: "You're the next big thing! You're this! You're that!" And you know, if you can anchor yourself in what is true, which is a form of spirituality for me, you can find out what is true. You don't get bitter, you don't get mad, you just say: "The truth to me is this—because I know it is so, and yes, you might turn to me today and say 'You're beautiful!', but you know what—I was beautiful yesterday, and the day before, and it's all from within me."

I go to a place called Agape, which is a non-denominational gathering of spiritual ideas of the old and new, and it's just a very warm place for me. It's a very *real* place for me. Agape, in Greek, means love; it's actually the love between man and God. I think the Greeks described three kinds of love; this is the highest form of love you can have, and that's what it's really about, love—and that, for me, is spirituality. If I can learn to love myself, without all the outside things that people put on you to say that say "Oh, because you're *this* way, you're beautiful", or because People magazine says you're one of the "50 Most Beautiful People"; if you can just put all of that in its place and realize it's just media, and that you are truly the embodiment of love, then you'll be fine. Sometimes it's hard! But that's when I have to keep going. You have to keep going back; you can't just take a hit and run. You have to keep it as part of your routine on a daily basis. I mean, you just get down on your knees, in a good old-fashioned way, and if it's your way, you *pray*! Every single day, I go out there, and I'm like: "See me through this day," and that's basically how I do it.

I think a lot of us do that, but not a lot of us talk about it, and not a lot of us are as eloquent in stating it that way...

There are people from all different sides of the fence in terms of this argument of spirituality, or some people call it religion, some people call it "I don't know". You have your Mel Gibsons of the world who have a story they want the world to see, and they have the medium to do it and proceed to do it their way. That's his choice. Then there are people who don't want to talk about it at all because it's not PC to even discuss it. I'm just who I am, and this is what I do, and I'm just going to be honest about it.

I think that one footnote to the whole thing, though, is that part of *keeping it real* and part of remembering who I am is also knowing that I'm fallible. That there will be times when I do slightly get "caught up", and I'll have to go back and check and say, "*Hey...*" There will be those times. But the key is how I deal with that "falling down". Do I beat myself up: "You're a bad person!" Or do I say, "You know what? I'm human; I made a mistake. I'm going to try and get back on track and move on." That's the biggest argument for me right now. It's realizing that when I *do* make mistakes, it's okay to make a mistake, and then get back on and keep going.

How important a concept in this business is "giving back"?

It's extremely important. When I was younger, I used to say, "There are certain occupations in the world that can be done away with and the world would still go on." And mine is one of those. People argue that entertainment is important, yes. There are different levels of entertainment, I do say that. We've become part of the fabric of society—that's the entertainment industry. I'm sure today, with the way we've been socialized, some people would probably *die* if there was no entertainment. But, in terms of basic human existence, and needs? It is what it is.

With that being said, we do perform a function in society. And as part of society, we need to be able to be in the fiber of it, like cogs in the wheel. And so we hold up different parts. The doctors, the teachers, everybody holds up their own part in society. That being said; it's a never-ending thing. We give, and it comes back.

You can give in different ways. I personally think that just going to work and putting out good messages on television is a way of giving back, but it's not enough for me. Especially coming from where I come from, and seeing what I've seen. I would like to be more hands-on, in the trenches; that's just who I am—*given the time*. Now, I kid you not, when I was NOT on television, I had a lot more time. Now that I have a regular gig, it's a lot harder for me to commit to that time factor. I couldn't imagine life without giving back, in some form, shape or size. I think it's because I recognize the need so clearly and also, just in the spiritual scheme of things, it's about balances. I am by no means an ardent Christian or anything like that, but I think there's a saying in the Bible that goes: "To whom much is given, much is expected", and much has been given to me...so automatically, I am giving back in the way that I can. It's just the way I've been brought up.

I feel like: If I were to die today, what would be my legacy? The millions of dollars that I could have made (which I haven't yet)? Or the property I might own? What is going to be my legacy? I would love for my legacy to be the fact that I might have helped one kid get out of trouble, move on and become a success in his life. So he can take a little bit of me with him and so when he sits down and talks to someone, he can say—even if he doesn't remember my name—he can turn around and say, "There was this one guy, who paid *that* much attention to me when I needed it, and he helped me through a hard time." I'm good. I'm happy for the rest of my eternity if that happens. Even just the once. I'm good. I'm straight. I don't need to worry about another thing because you know what—it's being passed on. And in Africa they say that it takes a village to raise a child, so it just spreads out. That, for me, is the key where all this is concerned. It's a community thing, a true community thing, in its truest form. Giving back is part of it.

How long have you been volunteering with at-risk or incarcerated juveniles; how did you get interested in that?

The first time I volunteered in America was with blind people, reading to them. Then I moved on to a children's camp in Brooklyn, NY to volunteer with them. Before that, actually years ago, I had come over on a program called "Camp Counselors from England", working with kids from the inner cities, and I fell in love with the kids. They were so beautiful and amazing; all they needed was a bit of attention. Flash forward to today, I was looking for another program to get involved with and the founder, Laura Leigh Hughes, came by Agape and she was being awarded with a donation and a plaque for contributing to the community toward peace and uplifting the community (with her project "The Unusual Suspects"). Afterward, they go outside and give information on their program, and hers just appealed to me. I went over and sat with her and we had an interview, and spoke for three hours. There is the issue of Black men and Latino young men, who, in society today, are almost like an endangered species. Statistics are kind of shocking, the amount of men of color who have been in prison or been in the system at some stage in their life. It's like, really shocking. It's a scary thing—once you get into the system, getting out is like taking superglue off your hands. It's just so hard...but it can be done. We go in and we work with these young men and women, and it's very, very, very rewarding. It's probably the most rewarding thing I've ever done in my life.

I got involved because I really wanted to be in the trenches; I really wanted to be in "the front", really seeing with my own two eyes—getting the true nuances of it: the smells, the touches, the feelings, all that type of stuff. I started doing it in the year 2000. I've been on a hiatus for a while, but I'm still involved with the organization. Matter of fact, next week there's a fundraiser that I'm going to attend.

Describe your work with "The Unusual Suspects":

In a nutshell, my breakdown of it would be that there are a bunch of professionals who work in the arts who would go into juvenile hall and meet with these young kids who are being rewarded; I guess it's kind of a reward for them to be in our program—because they're incarcerated and if they exhibit good behavior and do well, and trust me—kids are kids—they're going to act up anyway; they're just kids. We go in and we come up with ideas with the kids on writing a play; we write the play with them over a period of four months; we go in every Sunday and closer toward the play, we go in as many times as we can. We come up with a play, come up with the props, we bring in professionals to help with the props, with the set, with the costumes...but we literally take a back seat, a supervising back seat; we let them literally generate the whole process. We show them what it's like to go through the whole process, from the music to the writing to the directing to the blocking, everything. We put on a performance for their parents and their peers at the end of it.

To see their faces—when young guys play girls, or when they dress up as aliens, or they dress up as different characters and the commitment and the joy...the fact that they can just be kids again...And a lot of them stay in contact with us, they still write letters and say it's the best experience they've ever had in their life, and they've never seen anything like it. Some of these kids come out with words that society doesn't believe exist within them. They're really really smart kids. That's what we do.

Any insights about the role and nature of personal *character* in this business?

Personal character in this business? Some people would say you'd have to *not* have one to be successful in this business; I would beg to differ. If you can go home and sleep at night, because you know that you've been a decent person...I don't care how many millions you've been paid for it, if you've been an ass, you're an ass.

I've been really lucky to meet people who have put forth a good foot and they have great personal character. Now, that might be because they are just doing it with me; I don't think so, because I would say I am a pretty good judge of character. People are just such asses sometimes in the industry. When you hear "So-and-so is *so* bad or whatever..." I have, touch wood, never met one. I believe that what you put out is what you sometimes get.

I'll give you an example—there is a person in the industry who is notorious for being mean. I actually happen to know this person out of working situations. One time I had to meet with this person and the person was lacking in respect for my time, hugely lacking in respect for my time. But as soon as the person came out, nice as roses. Not to say that what they did was fine, but when they came to dealing with me face-to-face, nice as anything. I like to take that part of it away with me and leave the other part. But subsequently I've turned around to the people I work with and said, "I don't ever want to be in that situation again with that person." If I have to have a meeting with that person, I'll specifically make sure that that person knows that I have a hard out—that if I have a meeting with you at 1:00, I have to be out of there by 1:45, that kind of thing. All it takes is for my agent or manager to call up and say, "He has to be somewhere else by such-and-such a time." You find ways to protect yourself. In order to survive in this business you need not to let things hurt you. The funniest thing of all is for me to say that is kind of a really interesting contradiction because I'm the most sensitive person in the world. However, when it comes to certain things, I can draw the line in the sand and be like: "Okay! That's that, and this is this!"

People are as varied as grains of sand on the beach. There are going to be some who are up and some who are down, some who are happy and some who are sad. They were like that before they met you and will probably be like that after you meet them. If you can just be yourself and truly be the embodiment of who you are, which I hope is *love*—I think everybody is love—maybe you might teach that person something.

Just be yourself. If someone has that frantic energy, you don't take it on. You just breathe, and hold the arms on the arm chair and just keep a mild smile on your face. Don't be a grinning madman, but just a mild smile on your face; that might just soften them a bit, and you never know, they might go away and think about it twice. That's your legacy in life; you've made a difference.

CHAPTER TWELVE

YOU CAN NEVER REALLY GO BACK HOME

Home is where your life is. After six months or so of living in Los Angeles, you may begin to refer to it as *home*, and to where you came from as your "hometown". This is an important distinction. When you visit your hometown after beginning your Hollywood career, you may be regarded as a foreigner. Example: you may be referred to as "The Californian" when you go back to Toledo, and you may be referred to as "The Buckeye" when you are back in Los Angeles. This dichotomy will not last forever, as "Buckeye" will, over time, give way to "Angeleno". You need not abandon your roots, and you shouldn't, but understand that some subtle changes were taking place while you were settling in.

IMPERCEPTIBLE SHIFTS

Life in Los Angeles will change you in ways that you, yourself, will not be able to notice. The changes will have occurred so gradually as to be imperceptible to you. However, the folks in your hometown will see the end result of the changes, rather than the gradual assimilation of the changes. They might notice that you move faster, are more impatient in traffic, and talk a mile a minute (unless, of course, you are from New York, in which case, you will be perceived as moving slower, and speaking like you have a mouth full of molasses). You may stick out in your hometown with your newly adjusted sense of fashion. Face it folks, there ain't any horse shit on your cowboy boots no more. When you sit down to watch TV with your friends and family, you might personally know half of the people in the commercials ("He goes to my gym!"), and slowly you will realize that you are more connected than you thought you were.

People in your hometown may regard you differently, particularly as you build a career and experience success over time. They may treat you like a movie star, even if you are not. You are the closest thing they have ever experienced to a movie star. For God's sakes, you know movie stars *personally*, don't you? Alternatively, they may regard you, automatically, as one of "them" (particularly if you hail from Northern California, where disdain for Southern California is practically the law). People in your hometown may be intimidated by you, perceiving you as a powerful mover-and-shaker type, untouchable and influential. They may not trust you anymore, as you have lost your insider's hometown edge. These shifts are natural; the entertainment industry is a great mystery to those outside of it.

There may be some in your hometown who want to pick your brain like a vulture for details on life in Hollywood. They may seek your advice on their talent, they may be curious to know how life in the industry works, they may be looking for the inside "scoop" on some gossip item. Keep in mind that the things you consider quotidian, like Meg Ryan being in your yoga class, may be big news to folks in your hometown. They may have a hidden dream to pursue a career in entertainment. You're likely the closest link they have to the industry. Try to be gracious and answer their questions honestly; your opinions may carry more weight than you realize.

KEEPING A PIECE OF YOUR HOMETOWN IN YOUR POCKET

No matter where you have come from, you will always have a piece of your hometown in your consciousness, even if you hated living there. Embrace the influences that shaped you. Do not try to fight them or shut them down. The environment that created you will resonate forever in what you do. You will see echoes of your childhood, and the influences that shaped you, for years to come—reflected in the choices you make in life, even in your career. It is your responsibility to not lose touch with who you are and where you came from. Use the influences that surrounded you to amplify your personal stamp on your work.

Hollywood is a diverse community of individuals of different flavors, beliefs, accents and textures. Your unique hometown take on life has an important place in the industry. Your distinct cultural sensibilities will add perspective in the hurricane of showbiz. What you bring to the table from Buffalo, Des

Moines, Butte, or Tallahassee is part of the strength and breadth of our creative force that allows the industry to thrive.

You will undoubtedly have more people pulling for you from your hometown than you will ever know. You are not only living out your personal dreams in Hollywood, but you also carry the dreams of many of your teachers and guides on your shoulders. They had the skills to lead you, and you had the guts to follow your heart. People will look to you for inspiration, whether you accept the role or not. Kick ass, remembering that when you do, your entire hometown community does, too.

INTERVIEW

Subject: Beth McNamara
TV Producer
Credits include: ***American Idol***

Hometown: Holden, MA (pop. 16,000)
Moved to LA: 1989

Topic: You've Come A Long Way, Baby

How big a place is Holden, Massachusetts; what's it like?

Holden is the kind of town where you can ride your bike to the town pool and leave your front door open. The safety of my small town really allowed me the opportunity to be independent and extroverted. When my sister was pregnant with her first child I suggested she name him Holden…and she did.

When did you decide to move to LA?

I decided to move to LA my freshman year of college when I was attending Syracuse University. I wanted to study film & TV at a more metropolitan university, so I transferred to University of Southern California. The irony is that I went there to study film/TV, but decided to study International Relations because of my interest in global issues and the desire to go study abroad—I did a semester in Kenya.

Describe your first living arrangement in LA:

I lived in university housing with a roommate.

What was your first job/how did you get it?

My first paying job in the entertainment business was as a set dresser in the art department on the film *What's Eating Gilbert Grape* starring Johnny Depp and Leonardo DiCaprio. The movie was shot on location in Austin, TX, and in order to get the job I agreed to work as a local. My friend was living there, so for $100 a month I slept in the attic of the house he and his roommates were renting. No heat and only one light. Aaaah, in your youth you can tolerate a lot.

How did it feel to go back and visit, in the early days?

Going back to Holden after living in LA, I think the first thing that really hit me was how quiet it was at night and how early businesses close. At my 10-year high school reunion where most of my classmates were married and some even had 3 kids, I really felt different being a single career woman who, besides myself, only had one house plant to take care of.

When did you realize you referred to LA as "home"?

I think that I first referred to LA as home when I got married in 2002. My husband is also from Massachusetts, but we met in Los Angeles. For me, Los Angeles just felt like somewhere I lived and worked a lot, until I made my own home with my husband and two cats.

Was there a defining moment when you realized that you had changed, that you were different from the girl you were in Holden?

No. I don't really feel any different and I think that is because my parents raised me to be an individual with goals to lead, not follow, the crowd. I always did my own thing when I was young and living in a small town, and I am the same way now.

How often do you get to go home these days?

I go home once or twice a year, usually for holidays, and I like to drive by the house I grew up in on John Alden Road.

When did you realize that you were successful?

I think the time I first realized I was successful as a small town girl was when the city newspaper did a full page story on me and another local who work on *American Idol.* After the story ran, my parents got calls and emails from all kinds of people. My parents were so proud, which is a big part of success.

Do people in Holden treat you differently now?

My oldest friends still treat me the same, and since now I have lived in Los Angeles almost as many years as I did in Holden, I really don't keep in touch with very many people. There are lots of new people as the town has grown.

How much of the environment that shaped you do you carry in your pocket?

Growing up in Holden I was taught to always try my best, respect myself and others and give back to my community. I truly believe that my small town values are the foundation of my success in the entertainment business and in my personal life.

Any other insights you'd like to add?

I truly believe that no matter where you are from, you can pursue any dream you have. If you are interested in a career in medicine, go volunteer at a local hospital. If you want a career in television, get a summer internship at your local news station. You determine your future, so get off the couch or pick up the phone and take the first step—you will be surprised how a career path can just naturally fall into place once you take the first step.

I think the most important thing that I have learned working in the entertainment business is that professional success is worthless unless you are happy. It may sound trite, but I see examples of imbalance every day in my business.

APPENDICES

APPENDIX A—JOB LISTINGS

Department	The Line	Job Title	Domain	Job Responsibilities
Production	above	**Executive Producer**	F/TV	Executive from a studio or production company, overseeing development, production, post, and/or distribution of a project. Sometimes an independent financier, or an individual who has found substantial financing for a project
Production	above	**Producer**	F/TV/C	Individual who has substantially participated in the creation, development, production, marketing, sale or distribution of a project
Production	above	**Co-Producer**	F/TV	Individual who has participated in some aspect of development, production, or sale of a project
Production	above	**Associate Producer**	F/TV	Individual who, to a lesser degree than Co-Producer, has participated in some aspect of development, production, or sale of a project
Production	above	**Line Producer**	F/TV/C	On-Set Producer. Puts out all fires, deals with all problems of physical production, oversees budgetary concerns, oversees all employees, serves as liaison to Producer, Production Company and Studio
Production	above	**Creative Producer**	TV	Producer guiding creative aspects of production, including story, "look", and character development
Production	above	**Creator**	TV	Individual credited with creating or inventing the premise, characters, and basic storyline of the show
Production	above	**Writer**	F	The individual who wrote, or did rewrites on, the script
Production	above	**Writer**	TV	One of several people who collaborates on dialogue and plot for any given episode
Production	above	**Script Doctor**	F	An individual who does a punch-up on a script, changing the plot & dialog per studio notes
Production	above	**Director**	F/C	The individual whose storytelling vision is being realized, giving direction to actors and all creative deaprtment heads

Production	above	**Director**	TV	The individual who makes the writers' vision come to life, giving direction to actors, based on notes from writers and producers
Accounting	below	**Production Accountant**	F/TV/C	Peforms all production accounting duties except for payroll, writes checks, keeps budget logs on all departments
Accounting	below	**1st Assistant Accountant**	F/TV/C	Assists Accountant in all duties, performs overflow tasks
Accounting	below	**Accounting Assistant**	F/TV/C	Generally assists Accounting department
Art	below	**Production Designer**	F/TV/C	Designs the "look"—shape, size, feel—of the sets, scenery and physical objects on screen, sets color palette and mood
Art	below	**Art Director**	F/TV/C	Production Designer's "right-hand-man", fully assists in realization of design vision
Art	below	**Set Designer**	F/TV/C	Designs blueprints for construction of sets and other large objects that need to be built
Art	below	**Art Department Coordinator**	F/TV/C	Responsible for maintaining constant flow of work in and out of department, handles mostly paperwork and scheduling
Art	below	**Set Decorator**	F/TV/C	Furnishes the constructed set with items to enhance the design
Art	below	**Leadman**	F/TV/C	In charge of the Swing Gang, oversees assembly of sets
Art	below	**On-Set Dresser**	F/TV/C	Ensures continuity of all set-dressing items, moves furniture
Art	below	**Set Dresser**	F/TV/C	Assists Set Decorator in furnishing sets with decorative items
Art	below	**Swing gang**	F/TV/C	AKA Art Dogs; Assemble sets
Art	below	**Storyboard Artist**	F/TV/C	Creates illustrated frame-by-frame shot list, per director's vision
Art	below	**Prop Master**	F/TV/C	Responsible for purchasing, creation, renting, and continuity of all hand-props
Art	below	**Assistant Property Master**	F/TV/C	Assists the Prop Master in all duties
Art	below	**Weapons Wrangler, Weapons Handler**	F/TV/C	Must be licensed to possess and discharge firearms; handles, instructs, and supervises actors in use of weapons
Art	below	**Additional Props**	F/TV/C	Additional help to Prop Master
Art	below	**Construction Coordinator**	F/TV/C	Oversees all set and large object construction ordered by the art department
Art	below	**Construction Office Coordinator**	F/TV/C	Coordinates and schedules all construction, mostly via paperwork and phone, for art department

Art	below	**Labor Foreman**	F/TV/C	Oversees all work processes and laborers constructing sets, etc.
Art	below	**Scenic Artist**	F/TV/C	A specialty painter, skilled in faux finishes or age/tech work on surfaces
Art	below	**Painter**	F/TV/C	A person who executes the scenic artitst's painting techniques
Art	below	**Propmaker Foreman**	F/TV/C	Oversees all construction of hand-props
Art	below	**Propmaker**	F/TV/C	Constructs hand-props
Assistant Directors	below	**1st Assistant Director (1st AD)**	F/TV/C	Runs the set, schedules the production, sets the pace
Assistant Directors	below	**2nd Assistant Director (2nd AD)**	F/TV/C	Creates the call sheet, production reports, serves as a liaison from the production office to set, assists the 1st AD in running production smoothly
Assistant Directors	below	**2nd 2nd Assistant Director (2nd 2nd AD)**	F/TV/C	Liaison from base camp to set; walks actors from their trailers to set, assists 1st AD in running production smoothly
Assistant Directors	below	**DGA Trainee**	F/TV	Functions similarly to a PA, but is on set to observe and learn the production rythyms as part of their training in the Director's Guild program
Assistant Directors	below	**Set Production Assistant (PA)**	F/TV/C	Assists the 1st AD in running production smoothly
Assistant Directors	below	**Key Set Production Assistant (PA)**	F/TV/C	Head of the PAs, assists the 1st AD in running production smoothly
Camera	below	**Director of Photography (DP)**	F/TV/C	Designs all lighting schematics and directs camera movement for the project, sets mood with lighting, selects shots, angles and length of lens in coordination with Director's vision
Camera	below	**Director of Photography (DP)**	TV	In sit-com television, or otherwise staged television performance, designs, re-sets, and engineers overhead lighting grid to facilitate adequate lighting for good shots on three or four cameras at a time
Camera	below	**Camera Operator**	F/TV/C	Physically operates the camera, sits behind eyepiece and shoots film
Camera	below	**1st Assistant Camera (1st AC)**	F/TV/C	Pulls focus and measures focal lengths; places actors' marks in tape or other on floor
Camera	below	**2nd Assistant Camera (2nd AC)**	F/TV/C	Downloads and reloads camera with film, marks and claps the slate at the beginning of each take, keeps track of film totals
Camera	below	**B-Camera Operator**	F/TV/C	Additional camera operator
Camera	below	**Steadicam Operator**	F/TV/C	Specialty camera operator skilled in steadicam photography

Camera	below	**Loader**	F/TV/C	Loads film into magazines in a darkroom in the camera truck, keeps outgoing and incoming film footage tallies
Camera	below	**Video Playback**	F/TV/C	Converts 24fps film into 30 fps video so that when played back, does not flutter, operates playback system while shooting
Camera	below	**Video Assist**	F/TV/C	Sets up and maintains montiors linked directlly to camera so that director, producer, DP can watch what is being shot
Camera	below	**Unit Photographer**	F/TV/C	Takes still photographs for later use in publicity or promotion
Casting	below	**Casting Director**	F/TV/C	Brings in candidates for roles in the project, conducts auditions and meetings
Casting	below	**Casting Assistant**	F/TV/C	Assists the Casting Director, operates video camera to record auditions, reads lines with actors
Casting	below	**Extras Casting**	F/TV/C	Provides production with background players suitable to the project
Catering	below	**Caterer**	F/TV/C	Provides hot breakfast and lunch for crew, cooked on location in a catering truck, also provides tables, chairs, silverware, plates
Catering	below	**Chef**	F/TV/C	Creates menu for each meal, cooks and serves food to crew
Catering	below	**Assistant Cook**	F/TV/C	Assists chef in cooking and serving, helps to clean up
Catering	below	**Chef's Assistant**	F/TV/C	Assists chef in cooking and serving, helps to clean up
Choreography	below	**Choreographer**	F/TV/C	Creates dance steps and routines based on director's vision, teaches these steps to dancers and actors, conducts auditions and rehearsals
Choreography	below	**Assistant Choreographer**	F/TV/C	Assists choreographer in auditions and rehearsals, takes care of paperwork and technical details
Choreography	below	**Dance Instructor**	F/TV/C	Assists choreographer in rehearsals, teaching and reinforcing dance steps and routines
Choreography	below	**Stunt Spotter**	F/TV/C	Provides safety for dangerous or difficult dance moves, during rehearsals and shooting
Continuity	below	**Script Supervisor**	F/TV/C	Responsible for cataloguing all shots and angles, duration of scenes, screen direction, continutity for the entire shooting process
Costumes	below	**Costume Designer**	F/TV/C	Designs the "look" and personality of the characters through clothing and accessories
Costumes	below	**Costume Supervisor**	F/TV/C	Implements scheduling, breakdowns, budgets, and running of the wardrobe department—the "right-hand-man" to the costume designer

Costumes	below	**Key Set Costumer**	F/TV/C	Responsible for setting actors' clothing in their trailers, maintaining continuity books and continuity of clothing
Costumes	below	**Set Costumer**	F/TV/C	Responsible for setting actors' clothing in their trailers, maintaining continuity books and continuity of clothing
Costumes	below	**Ager-Dyer**	F/TV/C	Distresses, dyes, and paints wardrobe, fabric, and accessories to make them look old or worn
Costumes	below	**Assistant Costume Designer**	F/TV/C	Assists the costume designer in overflow duties—sourcing fabric & notions, setting up product placement
Costumes	below	**Costume Illustrator**	F/TV/C	Produces illustrations, per the costume designer's vision, of costumes to be worn in a project
Costumes	below	**Seamstress**	F/TV/C	Sews, alters, and repairs wardrobe
Costumes	below	**Additional Costumer**	F/TV/C	Usually responsible for dressing background extras, keeping continuity book and maintaining on-set continuity
Craft Service	below	**Craft Service**	F/TV/C	Provides food and beverages for the cast and crew on set at all times
Craft Service	below	**Assistant Craft Service**	F/TV/C	Assists the craft service person on set, performs shopping duties
Electric	below	**Chief Lighting Technician (Gaffer)**	F/TV/C	Consulting with Director of Photography, implements layout and tweaks all lighting setups
Electric	below	**Best Boy Electric**	F/TV/C	"Right-hand-man" to the Gaffer, helps to implement and install lighting setups
Electric	below	**Lighting Technician**	F/TV/C	Installs, sets up and operates lights and lighting designs per the Gaffer and Best Boy
Electric	below	**Lighting Board operator**	F/TV/C	Operates a dimmer board for special lighting effects
Electric	below	**Spot Operator**	F/TV/C	Operates a follow-spot spotlight
Grip	below	**Key Grip**	F/TV/C	Responsible for set-up, moving, implementation, and safety of all rigs on set, especially for camera and electric departments
Grip	below	**Best Boy Grip**	F/TV/C	"Right-hand-man" to the Key Grip, helps to design and implement rigs for use on set
Grip	below	**Dolly Grip**	F/TV/C	Sets up dolly on track, marks stop and start spots, pushes or pulls dolly to achieve tracking shots
Grip	below	**Grip**	F/TV/C	Implements rigging, set-up, moving, and safety for Camera and Electric departments on set
Grip	below	**Rigging Grip**	F/TV/C	Specifically hired to set up special camera or lighting rigs
Hair	below	**Head Hair Stylist**	F/TV/C	Responsible for the creation of hair styles for characters, and their continuity and maintenance on set

Hair	below	**Key Hair Stylist**	F/TV/C	Responsible for the daily styling of actors' hair, and the continuity and maintenance of hairstyles on set
Hair	below	**Hair Stylist**	F/TV/C	Responsible for the daily styling of actors' hair, and the continuity and maintenance of hairstyles on set
Locations	below	**Location Manager**	F/TV/C	Searches out, and photographs potential locations for shooting. Pulls permits, secures location, arranges for security, cast, crew and transportation set-up and shooting requirements.
Locations	below	**Assistant Location manager**	F/TV/C	Assists Location Manager in tracking down potential locations and permits
Make-up	below	**Make-up Designer**	F/TV/C	Responsible for creating make-up looks for characters, and the continuity and maintenance of the make-up on set
Make-up	below	**Key Make-up Artist**	F/TV/C	Responsible for applying make-up on actors at call time, and for ensuring make-up continuity and maintenance on set
Make-up	below	**Make-up Artist**	F/TV/C	Responsible for applying make-up on actors at call time, and for ensuring make-up continuity and maintenance on set
Music	below	**Composer**	F/TV/C	Composes music, in the form of a "score" to accompany moving images on screen
Music	below	**Music Supervisor**	F/TV	Supervises use and selection of pre-existing music for a project
Music	below	**Music Clearance**	F/TV	Obtains legal clearance to use pre-existing music for a project
Music	below	**Orchestrator**	F/TV	Arranges musical compositions for a performance group or orchestra
Post	below	**Editor**	F/TV/C	Cuts footage, edits film, sets emotional tone and pace of project
Post	below	**Assistant Editor**	F/TV/C	Assists editor in going through footage log, makes dubs of cut scenes to distribute to production
Post	below	**Post Production Supervisor**	F/TV	Oversees all aspects of post-production, including editing, sound design, music, for a project
Post	below	**Post Production Assistant (PA)**	F/TV	Serves as a gopher, runner, general office assistant to the Post Supervisor
Post	below	**Sound Editor**	F/TV	Edits sounds to make for clearer understanding of action, or to enhance impact of action on screen
Post	below	**Sound Designer**	F/TV	Designs "soundscapes", placing audience in the environment literally or emotionally represented on screen
Post	below	**Foley Artist**	F/TV	Performs sound replacement, sound effect or sound enhancement to accompany moving image
Production	below	**Unit Production Manager (UPM)**	F/TV/C	Manages production on-site, responsible for all departments and their budgets

Production	below	**Production Supervisor**	F/TV/C	Manages production usually in the production office, managing details and concerns of physical produciton
Production	below	**Production Coordinator (POC)**	F/TV/C	Works in Production Office as a liaison to the set, generating and maintaining crew and cast lists, following up on contracts, fielding calls and inquiries about the production, streamlining and organizing work processes
Production	below	**Assistant Production Coordinator (APOC)**	F/TV/C	Assists the Production Coordinator in all s/he does, fields phonecalls, helps to keep production organized
Production	below	**Office Production Assistant (PA)**	F/TV/C	Assists production from the office, making runs and deliveries, answering phones, etc.
Production	below	**Office Runner**	F/TV/C	Makes deliveries and pickups for production; courier
Production	below	**Assistant to the Producer**	F/TV/C	Handles paperwork and overflow for the Producer
Production	below	**Assistant to the Director**	F/TV/C	Handles Paperwork and overflow of non-production duties for the Director
Set	below	**Security**	F/TV/C	On-site security: 24 hours, usually out-sourced through a security company
Set	below	**Fire Safety Officer**	F/TV/C	AKA Fire Marshall—paid, off-duty fire personnel legally obligated to be hired for shooting days involving flame, fire, or pyrotechnics
Set	below	**Traffic Police**	F/TV/C	Paid, off-duty police officers (usually traffic officers) who direct, divert, and control the flow of traffic to enable shooting in the street or on the sidewalk
Set	below	**Set Medic**	F/TV/C	A certified Emergency Medical Technician, or Emergency Nurse, hired by production to take care of cast and crew in the event of illness or injury
Set	below	**Studio Teacher**	F/TV/C	A certified and credentialed teacher, responsible for tutoring and educating young actors (under age 18, or non-empancipated) and supervising their homework assignments
Sound	below	**Sound Mixer**	F/TV/C	An audio specialist who records production sound and dialog (with the assistance of a boom operator) on a mixing board
Sound	below	**Boom Operator**	F/TV/C	Operates a boom microphone, providing sound to the sound mixer
Sound	below	**Cable Wrangler**	F/TV/C	Responsible for gathering and letting out cable for the boom operator during tricky or dangerous sound setups
Special FX	below	**Special Effects Creator**	F/TV/C	Creates, designs and conceptualizes special effects, effects make-up and effects processes

Special FX	below	**Special Effects Designer**	F/TV/C	With FX Creator, designs special effects processes and effects make-up
Special FX	below	**Special Effects Make-up Artist**	F/TV/C	Applies makeup, prosthetics, and appliances to create special effects
Special FX	below	**Special Effects Moldmaker**	F/TV/C	Casts subjects' body parts for later sculpting and appliance creation, mixes foam latex, pours into molds, bakes appliance pieces
Special FX	below	**Special Effects Technician**	F/TV/C	Performs non-make-up effects, including puppetry work, robotics, animatronics
Special FX	below	**Special Effects Costumer**	F/TV/C	Constructs, fits, and maintains specialty and effects costumes
Special FX	below	**Robotics Engineer**	F/TV/C	Develops, engineers and implements robotic technology to facilitate special effects
Special FX	below	**Sculptor**	F/TV/C	Sculpts appliances for special effects make-up use, sculpts maquettes and creature effects
Special FX	below	**Mold Painter**	F/TV/C	Paints foam latex appliances to look real or believable for special effects
Special FX	below	**Pyrotechnics Designer**	F/TV/C	Designs, engineers, and supervises all aspects of pyrotechnics, including use of live flame, torches, and explosions
Special FX	below	**Pyrotechnics Technician**	F/TV/C	Implements, sets up, rigs and executes pyrotechnic events
Stunts	below	**Stunt Coordinator**	F/TV/C	Hires stunt performers, designs stunts and rigs to be performed safely on screen
Stunts	below	**Stunt/Fight Choreographer**	F/TV/C	Designs each specific movement in a fight sequence, rehearses with actors, supervises during shooting
Stunts	below	**Utility Stunt Performer**	F/TV/C	AKA Stuntman—performs stunts on screen
Stunts	below	**Stunt Double**	F/TV/C	A stunt performer, matching height/weight/body type of actor, for performing stunts when deemed too dangerous for the actor to perform
Stunts	below	**Specialty Stunt Performer**	F/TV/C	Stunt performer with special skills, ie: walking the high-wire, horse-back riding, gymnastics, juggling
Transportation	below	**Transportation Coordinator**	F/TV/C	Responsible for hiring drivers, leasing trailers, renting picture cars, and scheduling of all vehicular transportation
Transportation	below	**Transportation Captain**	F/TV/C	Oversees and supervises all movement in the transportation department; "right-hand-man" of the Transpo Coordinator
Transportation	below	**Honeywagon Driver**	F/TV/C	Drives, sets up, and maintains the honeywagon (large 2-piece trailer with rooms for several actors & public crew restrooms)

Transportation	below	**Production Van Driver**	F/TV/C	Shuttles crew and cast from parking to base camp, does runs when necessary
Transportation	below	**Driver**	F/TV/C	Performs any driving of vehicles necessary to production
Transportation	below	**Helicopter Pilot**	F/TV/C	Licensed helicopter pilot, flying for either on-screen production value, or to facilitate aerial photography
BIZ		**Agent: Above the Line**		Represents business interests of above-the-line clients, including actors, writers, producers and directors
BIZ		**Agent: Below the Line**		Represents business interests of below-the-line clients, including DPs, Editors, Production Designers, Costume Designers and Assistant Directors
BIZ		**Agent: Literary**		Represents the business interests of writer clients, for book, literary journal, magazine, and screenwriting placements
BIZ		**Agent: Packaging**		Assembles a "dream-team" of creative department heads for a project from the agency's existing client base
BIZ		**Agent's Assistant**		Assists agent, schedules meetings, fields phone calls, follows up with contracts, etc.
BIZ		**Manager**		Represents a clients long-term career interests, including creative alliances, career planning, development, networking, etc.
BIZ		**Manager's Assistant**		Assists manager, scheduling meetings, fielding phone calls, performing overflow duties
BIZ		**Publicist**		Seeks publicity for their clients in magazines, TV, journals and books; spins bad events into good events, performs "damage control" when necessary, generates professional interest in client and their work
BIZ		**Publicist's Assistant**		Assists publicist, scheduling meetings, parties, fielding phone calls, performing overflow duties
BIZ		**Accountant**		Performs accounting duties for clients, including bill payment, extimated tax payment, mortgage payment, etc.
BIZ		**Entertainment Lawyer**		Negotiates contracts for persons and companies involved in the entertainment industry
BIZ		**Creative Executive**		Executive from a studio or production company who seeks out new scripts to tweak and develop for their company, actively participates in script re-writes and streamlining story

BIZ		**Development Executive**		Executive representing studio or production company in charge of readying the project for production, finding or attaching interested actors and directors, and polishing the project
BIZ		**Network Executive**	TV	Executive representing the network's interest and programming desires in a television program
BIZ		**Production Executive**		Executive from a studio or production company overseeing physical production of a project
BIZ		**Acquisitions Executive**		Executive from a studio or distribution company who seeks out and purchases completed projects for distribution
BIZ		**Distributions Executive**		Executive from a studio or distribution company responsible for charting out, planning for release, and executing distribution of projects
BIZ		**Marketing Executive**		Executive from a studio or distribution company in charge of marketing and promoting projects that are being released
BIZ		**Financial Executive**		Executive from studio or other company in charge of charting, analyzing and planning financial moves beneficial to the company, overseeing all financial inflow and outflow for the company
BIZ		**Payroll Officer**		Individual in charge of timecard receipt, payroll accounting, and distribution of payroll checks to production
BIZ		**Bond Company Executive**		Executive in charge of overseeing a project on behalf of the bond company, would take over the project in case of major budget overage or force majeure incident
BIZ		**Union Business Agent**		Individual who "runs" a local division of a union, represents all union employees involved in labor disputes, negotiates union contracts with Producers Guild, oversees membership

APPENDIX B— RECOMMENDED READING

Hollywood Creative Directory: Spring 2004, 50th Edition
By Hollywood Creative Directory, February 2004

Hollywood Representation Directory
By Hollywood Creative Directory, December 2003

NFT Not For Tourists: Guide to Los Angeles
By Happy Mazza Media LLC; spiral-bound edition January 2003

Hello, He Lied
By Lynda Obst; Broadway, reprint edition September, 1997

Screenplay: The Foundations of Screenwriting; A step-by-step guide from concept to finished script
By Syd Field; DTP, 3rd edition June, 1984

Is That a Gun in Your Pocket?: Women's Experience of Power in Hollywood
By Rachel Abramowitz; Random House, 2000

Story: Substance, Structure, Style and the Principles of Screenwriting
By Robert McKee; Regan Books, 1st edition December 1997

ACKNOWLEDGEMENTS

This book could not have been written without help and support from the following individuals. I extend my most sincere gratitude to these wonderful people:

Reading, Editing & Mark-up: Kenneth White, Bridget Davis, Kali Sabnis Plomin, Garet Reilly, Ben Cook, Erin Podbereski, Rachael Leigh Cook, & Joseph E. Mullin

Interviewees: Claire Best, Mike Dougherty, Jon Favreau, Daniel Gillies, Jordan Levine, Mark Anthony Little, Beth McNamara, Anurag Mehta, Anthony Okungbowa, Todd Quinn, Jennifer Sanger, Holly Wiersma, & Denise Wingate

Technical Support: Lisa M. Jones, Amy Adams, Kevin Burke, Jason71 Pickersgill, Sam Adan and the crew at CRC, E. Marie Mullin, Richard Mullin

Information Gathering & Verification: Paul Sessum, Michael Vasquez, Sandra Marsh Management, Diana Qasabian-Bedrosian, Kimberly and David Smiler, Holly Keenan, Darren LeGallo

My teachers: Virgil C. Johnson, H. D. Motyl, Zack Kincheloe & Bobbi Nesteby

Life Support: Patricia Burke, Karen Hillman Fried, Anne Tolpegin, & Ryan Gosling.

CREDITS:

On the Front Cover: Amy Adams and Kevin Burke

On the Back Cover: Amy Adams

Cover Photos, Jennifer Sanger & Claire Best Photos: Lisa M. Jones

Graphic Design, LA Map and Covers: Jason71 Pickersgill

Anurag Mehta, Beth McNamara, Daniel Gillies, Todd Quinn, Jordan Levine Photos: Kristin Burke

Mike Dougherty photo courtesy of Mike Dougherty

Jon Favreau photo courtesy of Spencer Baumgarten, Endeavor

Mark Anthony Little Photo: Vera White

Tony Okungbowa Photo: Andrew McPherson, courtesy of Tony Okungbowa

Denise Wingate Photo: Alex Wright

Holly Wiersma Photo: Jeff Vespa/WireImage.com

AUTHOR'S NOTE:

No compensation whatsoever was given to the author for endorsement of any product, store, service, or facility mentioned herein.

ABOUT THE AUTHOR

Subject: Kristin M. Burke
Costume Designer, Author
Titles Include: *Running Scared, The Cooler, The Slaughter Rule* (CD);
Costuming for Film: the Art and the Craft (Co-Author)
Hometown: Chico, CA
Moved to LA: 1991

Educated at Northwestern University in Evanston, Illinois, Ms. Burke has designed costumes for more than thirty-five feature films, and she has also designed costumes for music videos, commercials, and two television series. In addition, she is an internationally-exhibited artist, specializing in collage and mail art, and had her first solo exhibition in Los Angeles in September, 2001.

Ms. Burke's first book, *Costuming for Film: the Art and the Craft,* is available from Silman James Press in September, 2004.

She lives in Los Angeles.

0-595-32495-9

CPSIA information can be obtained
at www.ICGtesting.com
Printed in the USA
FSHW021541260220
67562FS

9 780595 324958